An End Times ~~Pen~~ Reed

Learning the Stroke of His Genius

By: Moses Mo'Shay

Table of Contents:

Letter of Introduction

Matthew 20:23 KJV
Zechariah 4:11-14 KJV
Malachi 3:2-4 KJV

Behold, I will send my messenger, and he shall
prepare the way before me: and the LORD, whom ye seek,
shall suddenly come to his temple, even the messenger of the
covenant, whom ye delight in: behold, he shall come, saith the LORD
of hosts (Malachi 3:1 KJV). And I will come near to you to
judgment; And I will be a swift witness against the sorcerers, and
Against the adulterers, and against false swearers, and against those
that oppress the hireling in his wages, the widow, and the
fatherless, and that turn aside the stranger from his right, and fear
not me, saith the LORD of hosts (Malachi 3:5 KJV).
Then I turned, and lifted up mine eyes, and looked, and behold
A flying roll. And he said unto me, What seest thou? And I answered,
I see a flying roll; the length thereof is twenty cubits, and the
Breadth thereof ten cubits (Zechariah 5:1-2 KJV).
Then said he unto me, This is the curse that goeth forth over the face
of the whole earth: for every one that stealeth shall be cut off as
on this side according to it; and every one that sweareth
shall be cut off as on that side according to it.
I will bring forth, saith the LORD of hosts, and it
shall enter into the house of the thief, and into the house of him
that sweareth falsely by my name: and it shall remain in the midst
of his house, and shall consume it with the timber thereof and
the stones thereof (Zechariah 5:3-4 KJV)."

Sitting at the Left,
Moses, Mo'Shay

Warning!

The contents of these messages are highly extensive,
With shocking waves of resurrection that are divinely offensive.

From the beginning, there was a name and it has yet to be adorned,
A name within itself is a prophecy that warned.

About the lie that works against His holy truth of perfection,
A tongue that is deceived fares with a lying projection.

A tongue that is deceived takes with it souls that's left in mourning.
A dying world that needs "proof" should consider this fair warning.

Warning

What will ye? shall I come unto you with a rod, or in love, and in the spirit of meekness? (1 Corinthians 4:21 KJV)? Now I tell you before it come, that, when it is come to pass, ye may believe that I am he. Verily, verily, I say unto you, He that receiveth whomsoever I send receiveth me; and he that receiveth me receiveth him that sent me (John 13:19-20 KJV)." When the LORD thy God shall bring thee into the land whither thou goest to possess it, and hath cast out many nations before thee, the Hittites, and the Girgashites, and the Amorites, and the Canaanites, and the Perizzites, and the Hivites, and the Jebusites, seven nations greater and mightier than thou; And when the LORD thy God shall deliver them before thee; thou shalt smite them, and utterly destroy them; thou shalt make no covenant with them, nor shew mercy unto them: Neither shalt thou make marriages with them; thy daughter thou shalt not give unto his son, nor his daughter shalt thou take unto thy son (Deuteronomy 7:1-3 KJV).

If thou shalt say in thine heart, These nations are more than I; how can I dispossess them? Thou shalt not be afraid of them: but shalt well remember what the LORD thy God did unto Pharaoh, and unto all Egypt; The great temptations which thine eyes saw, and the signs, and the wonders, and the mighty hand, and the stretched out arm, whereby the LORD thy God brought thee out: so shall the LORD thy God do unto all the people of whom thou art afraid. Moreover the LORD thy God will send the hornet among them, until they that are left, and hide themselves from thee, be destroyed. Thou shalt not be affrighted at them: for the LORD thy God is among you, a mighty God and terrible (Deuteronomy 7:17-21 KJV). And the LORD thy God will put out those nations before thee by little and little: thou mayest not consume them at once, lest the beasts of the field increase upon thee. But the LORD thy God shall deliver them unto thee, and shall destroy them with a mighty destruction, until they be destroyed (Deuteronomy 7:22-23 KJV).

Fruit of the Spirit: **Goodness & Gentleness**

And he said, I will make all my goodness pass before thee, and I will proclaim the name of the LORD before thee; and will be gracious to whom I will be gracious, and will shew mercy on whom I will shew mercy (Exodus 33:19 KJV).

But the fruit of the Spirit is love, joy, peace, longsuffering, **gentleness**, **goodness**, faith, Meekness, temperance: against such there is no law (Galatians 5:22-23 KJV).

Mo'Shay

There's a difference in the sound; the name's not like it's spelled.
The pen name reads as Moses Moses; unique spelling has not failed.

Since I changed the way it's spelled, did the spelling change the meaning?
I thought with understanding, without my own that I was leaning.

In Hebrew it's Moshé; it's spelled the way my wording sounds.
He said the two are not at odds; they're even ~~keel~~ kill, so what's profound?

They say I know Your name and the way that it's pronounced.
I know that You're the way and weighed my options, so I bounced.

I bounced to go Your way. I bounced to this new beat.
I bounced to certain soundness; wrote this dance then took my seat.

Some say it wrong but live it right. Who says it right, but lives it wrong?
If you still don't know His name, it's in the life that's of this song.

If you still can't find it here, it's in the seeds that you have sown.
And if you still can't find it there, it's in the life that's not your own.

They claim my tongue's not of their mother; to that I say touché!
If history doesn't repeat itself, well then, my name is not Mo'Shay!

Mo' shay

There is an evil which I have seen under the sun, as an error which proceedeth from the ruler: Folly is set in great dignity, and the rich sit in low place. I have seen servants upon horses, and princes walking as servants upon the earth (Ecclesiastes 10:5-7 KJV). Now it came to pass in the days of Ahasuerus, (this is Ahasuerus which reigned, from India even unto Ethiopia, over an hundred and seven and twenty provinces:) That in those days, when the king Ahasuerus sat on the throne of his kingdom, which was in Shushan the palace, In the third year of his reign, he made a feast unto all his princes and his servants; the power of Persia and Media, the nobles and princes of the provinces, being before him: When he shewed the riches of his glorious kingdom and the honour of his excellent majesty many days, even an hundred and fourscore days (Esther 1:1-4 KJV).

Where were white, green, and blue, hangings, fastened with cords of fine linen and purple to silver rings and pillars of marble: the beds were of gold and silver, upon a pavement of red, and blue, and white, and black, marble. And they gave them drink in vessels of gold, (the vessels being diverse one from another,) and royal wine in abundance, according to the state of the king. And the drinking was according to the law; none did compel: for so the king had appointed to all the officers of his house, that they should do according to every man's pleasure (Esther 1:6-8 KJV). Lo, this is the man that made not God his strength; but trusted in the abundance of his riches, and strengthened himself in his wickedness (Psalm 52:7 KJV)." Their heart is as fat as grease; but I delight in thy law (Psalm 119:70 KJV). Jesus answered and said unto them, Ye do err, not knowing the scriptures, nor the power of God (Matthew 22:29 KJV).

Vashti

Deny the male called king. I'm feeling kind of bold.
She was a king within her rights, manifesting Manifold's.

Sometimes you'll make the right choice, and you'll lose your prized position.
You'll stand to hear a strange demand and understand His proposition.

Men of low degree rank high but know that looks can be deceiving.
In the balances are measures, but their weight is non-receiving.

They trusted in oppression and denied themselves a wealth.
They deceived themselves by law; bylaws are known to teach by stealth.

They were crying out from pride; pride comes forth before destruction.
She left based off demand, but she obeyed the right instructions.

If Wisdom's sounding cheeky, check your ears—they might be clogged.
Turn not right, nor to the left, but read right through this left-hand fog.

The lack of knowing has its privileges, yet I know something they don't.
They claim to be of certain service, but their actions say I won't.

True servants will be first, while wicked leaders working lastly.
Who will operate as one? He calls His humble servants Vashti!

Vashti

Doth not wisdom cry? and understanding put forth her voice? She standeth in the top of high places, by the way in the places of the paths. She crieth at the gates, at the entry of the city, at the coming in at the doors. Unto you, O men, I call; and my voice is to the sons of man. O ye simple, understand wisdom: and, ye fools, be ye of an understanding heart. Hear; for I will speak of excellent things; and the opening of my lips shall be right things. For my mouth shall speak truth; and wickedness is an abomination to my lips. All the words of my mouth are in righteousness; there is nothing froward or perverse in them. They are all plain to him that understandeth, and right to them that find knowledge. Receive my instruction, and not silver; and knowledge rather than choice gold. For wisdom is better than rubies; and all the things that may be desired are not to be compared to it (Proverbs 8:1-11 KJV).

I wisdom dwell with prudence, and find out knowledge of witty inventions. The fear of the LORD is to hate evil: pride, and arrogancy, and the evil way, and the froward mouth, do I hate. Counsel is mine, and sound wisdom: I am understanding; I have strength. By me kings reign, and princes decree justice. By me princes rule, and nobles, even all the judges of the earth. I love them that love me; and those that seek me early shall find me. Riches and honour are with me; yea, durable riches and righteousness. My fruit is better than gold, yea, than fine gold; and my revenue than choice silver. I lead in the way of righteousness, in the midst of the paths of judgment: That I may cause those that love me to inherit substance; and I will fill their treasures. The LORD possessed me in the beginning of his way, before his works of old (Proverbs 8:12-22 KJV).

Dance with Me

There's a dance that we can do, and this is how the dancing goes:
Forgive me ahead of time, I'm known for stepping on one's toes.

Should I allow you to see your way if you're ignoring other's needs?
You've cut yourself off from Me, but only to harvest a crop of weeds.

There's no easy way of death and there's no easy way to suffer.
There were two paths that you could take, and you decided on the rougher.

What is darkness but a veil; a common veil to those who perish.
This is not My will for you. Let these words be yours to cherish.

This is not a message of gloom, but surely one that's known as critical.
This is a creative way to guide; it leaves my prophet analytical.

Can you hear and see My love for you? This is no time to feel rejected.
This is the way of "Valor's" life, and opportunity to stand corrected.

This message may be hard to take, but who's to say that one's not gentle?
If you learn to hear My truths, you'll lose the mind that's mental.

God is preparing the "body" for burial. Who will rise as resurrected?
Those who danced to certain death and see their lives as being perfected.

Dance with Me

…Salvation to our God which sitteth upon the throne, and unto the Lamb (Revelation 7:10 KJV)!" …What are these which are arrayed in white robes? and whence came they? And I said unto him, Sir, thou knowest. And he said to me, These are they which came out of great tribulation, and have washed their robes, and made them white in the blood of the Lamb (Revelation 7:13-14 KJV). …It was before the LORD, which chose me before thy father, and before all his house, to appoint me ruler over the people of the LORD, over Israel: therefore will I play before the LORD. And I will yet be more vile than thus, and will be base in mine own sight… (2 Samuel 6:21-22 KJV)." … sorrow is turned into joy before him (Job 41:22 KJV). Let no man deceive himself. If any man among you seemeth to be wise in this world, let him become a fool, that he may be wise (1 Corinthians 3:18 KJV). The heart of the wise is in the house of mourning; but the heart of fools is in the house of mirth (Ecclesiastes 7:4 KJV).

I will build you up again, and you, Virgin Israel, will be rebuilt. Again you will take up your timbrels and go out to dance with the joyful (Jeremiah 31:4 KJV). And I heard a voice from heaven saying unto me, Write, Blessed are the dead which die in the Lord from henceforth: Yea, saith the Spirit, that they may rest from their labours; and their works do follow them (Revelation 14:13 KJV). Here is the patience of the saints: here are they that keep the commandments of God, and the faith of Jesus (Revelation 14:12 KJV). Fret not thyself because of evildoers, neither be thou envious against the workers of iniquity. For they shall soon be cut down like the grass, and wither as the green herb. Trust in the LORD, and do good; so shalt thou dwell in the land, and verily thou shalt be fed (Psalm 37:1-3 KJV). What shall I render unto the LORD for all his benefits toward me? I will take the cup of salvation, and call upon the name of the LORD. I will pay my vows unto the LORD now in the presence of all his people (Psalm 116:12-14 KJV).

God's Plan of Salvation
GPS

You often ask how I felt when I walked across the stage.
I felt that I was done but unfinished with the gauge.

God has a plan and an illogical navigation;
To free you from your passions full of toil and agitation.

Although you have come upon a stage that is completed,
There's a road that is called life, so do not exit on depleted.

Depleted is a road that has a speed without a bound,
So be patient as you listen so that your destiny is found.

Who can forget your hand at work, if inheriting the land re-minds?
Who's driving down a road where certain flags are known as signs?

Certain looks have killed true vision; I call the looks red flags.
Their covenant is unfamiliar, so it cannot help but nag.

Insight: Isaiah 30:15-17 MSG

It nags for you to save yourself; it nags you with its wisdom.
The way He leads may not make sense, but He'll guide you with His Is-dom.

God's Plan of Salvation
GPS

Listen, O isles, unto me; and hearken, ye people, from far; The LORD hath called me from the womb; from the bowels of my mother hath he made mention of my name. And he hath made my mouth like a sharp sword; in the shadow of his hand hath he hid me, and made me a polished shaft; in his quiver hath he hid me; And said unto me, Thou art my servant, O Israel, in whom I will be glorified. Then I said, I have laboured in vain, I have spent my strength for nought, and in vain: yet surely my judgment is with the LORD, and my work with my God. And now, saith the LORD that formed me from the womb to be his servant, to bring Jacob again to him, Though Israel be not gathered, yet shall I be glorious in the eyes of the LORD, and my God shall be my strength. And he said, It is a light thing that thou shouldest be my servant to raise up the tribes of Jacob, and to restore the preserved of Israel: I will also give thee for a light to the Gentiles, that thou mayest be my salvation unto the end of the earth. (Isaiah 49:1-6 KJV)."

Thus saith the LORD, the Redeemer of Israel, and his Holy One, to him whom man despiseth, to him whom the nation abhorreth, to a servant of rulers, Kings shall see and arise, princes also shall worship, because of the LORD that is faithful, and the Holy One of Israel, and he shall choose thee. Thus saith the LORD, In an acceptable time have I heard thee, and in a day of salvation have I helped thee: and I will preserve thee, and give thee for a covenant of the people, to establish the earth, to cause to inherit the desolate heritages; That thou mayest say to the prisoners, Go forth; to them that are in darkness, Shew yourselves. They shall feed in the ways, and their pastures shall be in all high places. They shall not hunger nor thirst; neither shall the heat nor sun smite them: for he that hath mercy on them shall lead them, even by the springs of water shall he guide them. And I will make all my mountains a way, and my highways shall be exalted. (Isaiah 49:7-11 KJV).

Consequential Conscience

Certain consequences had left me wallowing in sin;
It ended with His presence, so now where do I begin?

I had lost my confidence, because I dabbled in a pleasure.
My question had become a fleeting thought, what did I treasure?

I thought about my choices. What would the consequences be?
There was a fear that was within that held what truth had meant to me.

There was no one to blame. I knew that the fault was mine.
Would I really change the curve if I could put it in a line?

I thought, *Have pity on me, LORD. Wash away this guilty mind!*
I can overcome this sin, if you would only be so kind.

In the midst of it all, I felt a certain kind of peace.
What do you call a house that was never meant to lease?

What abounded had me troubled. Could I look Him in the face?
Some would say "how could you?" but by faith, I stand with grace.

Consequential Conscience

The law of the LORD is perfect, converting the soul: the testimony of the LORD is sure, making wise the simple. The statutes of the LORD are right, rejoicing the heart: the commandment of the LORD is pure, enlightening the eyes. The fear of the LORD is clean, enduring for ever: the judgments of the LORD are true and righteous altogether. More to be desired are they than gold, yea, than much fine gold: sweeter also than honey and the honeycomb. Moreover by them is thy servant warned: and in keeping of them there is great reward. Who can understand his errors? cleanse thou me from secret faults. Keep back thy servant also from presumptuous sins; let them not have dominion over me: then shall I be upright, and I shall be innocent from the great transgression. Let the words of my mouth, and the meditation of my heart, be acceptable in thy sight, O LORD, my strength, and my redeemer (Psalm 19:7-14 KJV).

Blessed are they that do his commandments, that they may have right to the tree of life, and may enter in through the gates into the city. For without are dogs, and sorcerers, and whoremongers, and murderers, and idolaters, and whosoever loveth and maketh a lie (Revelation 22:14-15 KJV) The LORD liveth; and blessed be my rock; and exalted be the God of the rock of my salvation. It is God that avengeth me, and that bringeth down the people under me. And that bringeth me forth from mine enemies: thou also hast lifted me up on high above them that rose up against me: thou hast delivered me from the violent man. Therefore I will give thanks unto thee, O LORD, among the heathen, and I will sing praises unto thy name. He is the tower of salvation for his king: and sheweth mercy to his anointed, unto David, and to his seed for evermore (2 Samuel 22:47-51 KJV). Now unto him that is able to keep you from falling, and to present you faultless before the presence of his glory with exceeding joy, To the only wise God our Saviour, be glory and majesty, dominion and power, both now and ever. Amen (Jude 1:24-25 KJV).

Is it Legible?

How do you explain how some stay stuck in what's corrupt?
He concealed His ways from the all-knowing, and so let me be abrupt.

If you cannot see the name, your law has made the eyes ineligible.
If you can hear me speak His way, that means His syllables are legible.

If you didn't get the name, then it's revealed within another.
What's unsightly of a nature that is common to your brother?

The eyes of man cannot see what Thee I Am has shown right through.
I ignore the rule of correctness; hereby, I Am is watching you.

If the wicked will not stand, what does it mean to be pronounced?
I pronounce within a judgment and may resemble what's denounced.

Who's for the juxtaposition of the opposition toward the supposition of Christ?
This was the blood that was shed that can never be priced!

And so, an image has a mystery and goes to measure with a reed.
Another image speaks in "tongues" to a servant who can read.

Is it Legible?

Because of the savour of thy good ointments thy name is as ointment poured forth, therefore do the virgins love thee (Song of Solomon 1:3 KJV). At that time Jesus answered and said, I thank thee, O Father, Lord of heaven and earth, because thou hast hid these things from the wise and prudent, and hast revealed them unto babes. Even so, Father: for so it seemed good in thy sight (Matthew 11:25-26 KJV). The heavens declare the glory of God; and the firmament sheweth his handywork. Day unto day uttereth speech, and night unto night sheweth knowledge. There is no speech nor language, where their voice is not heard. Their line is gone out through all the earth, and their words to the end of the world. In them hath he set a tabernacle for the sun, Which is as a bridegroom coming out of his chamber, and rejoiceth as a strong man to run a race. His going forth is from the end of the heaven, and his circuit unto the ends of it: and there is nothing hid from the heat thereof. The law of the LORD is perfect, converting the soul: the testimony of the LORD is sure, making wise the simple (Psalm 19:1-7 KJV).

For thus saith the Lord GOD, the Holy One of Israel; In returning and rest shall ye be saved; in quietness and in confidence shall be your strength: and ye would not. But ye said, No; for we will flee upon horses; therefore shall ye flee: and, We will ride upon the swift; therefore shall they that pursue you be swift. One thousand shall flee at the rebuke of one; at the rebuke of five shall ye flee: till ye be left as a beacon upon the top of a mountain, and as an ensign on an hill (Isaiah 30:15-17 KJV)." Some trust in chariots, and some in horses: but we will remember the name of the LORD our God (Psalm 20:7 KJV). And in his name shall the Gentiles trust. (Matthew 12:21 KJV).

Who Wants Hope?

I remember thinking that I didn't want this hope.
I wanted knowledge and clear vision, but the thought was just a joke.

Did it apply to wishful thinking? I didn't understand the term.
What was the substance of my hope? What was the key I had to learn?

Where did my faith lie that it would try to kill my spirit?
If He told me what it was, would I believe Him or just fear it?

Faith is the evidence of what doesn't appear to be so.
What appeared to be the truth was a falsehood saying no.

False affirmations make your purpose ineffective.
You will only hope in vain if your hearing is selective.

Would you want this hope if it denied you your own name?
Who wants hope; a pure hope that causes faith in you to wane?

Who Wants Hope?

I Am the man that hath seen affliction by the rod of his wrath. He hath led me, and brought me into darkness, but not into light. Surely against me is he turned; he turneth his hand against me all the day. My flesh and my skin hath he made old; he hath broken my bones. He hath builded against me, and compassed me with gall and travail. He hath set me in dark places, as they that be dead of old. He hath hedged me about, that I cannot get out: he hath made my chain heavy (Lamentations 3:1–7 KJV). He was unto me as a bear lying in wait, and as a lion in secret places. He hath turned aside my ways, and pulled me in pieces: he hath made me desolate. He hath bent his bow, and set me as a mark for the arrow. He hath caused the arrows of his quiver to enter into my reins. I was a derision to all my people; and their song all the day. He hath filled me with bitterness, he hath made me drunken with wormwood (Lamentations 3:10- 15 KJV).

Remembering mine affliction and my misery, the wormwood and the gall. My soul hath them still in remembrance, and is humbled in me. This I recall to my mind, therefore have I hope. It is of the LORD's mercies that we are not consumed, because his compassions fail not. They are new every morning: great is thy faithfulness. The LORD is my portion, saith my soul; therefore will I hope in him. The LORD is good unto them that wait for him, to the soul that seeketh him. It is good that a man should both hope and quietly wait for the salvation of the LORD. It is good for a man that he bear the yoke in his youth. He sitteth alone and keepeth silence, because he hath borne it upon him. He putteth his mouth in the dust; if so be there may be hope. He giveth his cheek to him that smiteth him: he is filled full with reproach. For the LORD will not cast off for ever (Lamentations 3:19-31 KJV).

The Secret to Submission

I didn't want to give up on all my desires.
I expressed my thoughts out loud, but they whispered back as liars.

I'm drowning in my sins, and my arms are surely flailing.
My spirit has been willing, but my flesh just keeps on failing.

If my flesh is weak, why does it overpower me?
I'm lighter than a feather, so it's my strength I do not see.

I couldn't seem to find the answer. Why wouldn't I just submit?
I saw myself as guilty; but it's my soul that you acquit.

Reference: 1 Corinthians 14:20 KJV

Was I as innocent as the children when it came to certain evil?
I was tried as an adult, but the indictment wasn't legal.

He said the secrets timely, but my lateness wouldn't show it.
If I said you heard the secret, would your eyes say I don't know it?

The Secret to Submission

The secret of the LORD is with them that fear him; and he will shew them his covenant (Psalm 25:14 KJV). The Lord GOD hath given me the tongue of the learned, that I should know how to speak a word in season to him that is weary: he wakeneth morning by morning, he wakeneth mine ear to hear as the learned. The Lord GOD hath opened mine ear, and I was not rebellious, neither turned away back. I gave my back to the smiters, and my cheeks to them that plucked off the hair: I hid not my face from shame and spitting. For the Lord GOD will help me; therefore shall I not be confounded: therefore have I set my face like a flint, and I know that I shall not be ashamed. He is near that justifieth me; who will contend with me? let us stand together: who is mine adversary? let him come near to me. Behold, the Lord GOD will help me; who is he that shall condemn me? lo, they all shall wax old as a garment; the moth shall eat them up (Isaiah 50:4-9 KJV)!

Who is among you that feareth the LORD, that obeyeth the voice of his servant… (Isaiah 50:10 KJV)? For when we were yet without strength, in due time Christ died for the ungodly. For scarcely for a righteous man will one die: yet peradventure for a good man some would even dare to die. But God commendeth his love toward us, in that, while we were yet sinners, Christ died for us. Much more then, being now justified by his blood, we shall be saved from wrath through him (Romans 5:6-9 KJV). Who is among you that feareth the LORD, that obeyeth the voice of his servant, that walketh in darkness, and hath no light? let him trust in the name of the LORD, and stay upon his God. Behold, all ye that kindle a fire, that compass yourselves about with sparks: walk in the light of your fire, and in the sparks that ye have kindled. This shall ye have of mine hand; ye shall lie down in sorrow. (Isaiah 50:10-11 KJV).

Fruit of the Spirit: **LOVE**

Whoso loveth instruction loveth knowledge: but he that hateth reproof is brutish. He that spareth his rod hateth his son: but he that loveth him chasteneth him betimes (Proverbs 12:1 & Proverbs 13:24 KJV).

All-Embracing

I'm an incomplete sentence of oxymorons.
I might confuse a certain ~~meddle~~ with metal(?) and call it Boron.

Who's a definition of a word they wouldn't look-up.
If you met your better half, would you likely hook-up?

Who thought outside the box was somewhere in the middle?
Attributed, attribute it; can you hear the riddle?

If I called King James a "mark" have I belittled?
I'm likely to tell him to practice second fiddle.

Insight: Romans 12:9-10 KJV

What kind of rain am I if I refuse to dribble?
When tenses are without agreement, I will call it scribble.

I am without a field of study, yet, I'm of a science.
The accent marks the spot, but not without reliance.

Is all or nothing sounding more like a threatening bully?
What's weighty about this message since you act like the pulley?

If all are not included, what am I defacing?
I'm known to incorrect your truths, and so, who's all-embracing?

All-Embracing

Even to day is my complaint bitter: my stroke is heavier than my groaning. Oh that I knew where I might find him! that I might come even to his seat! I would order my cause before him, and fill my mouth with arguments. I would know the words which he would answer me, and understand what he would say unto me. Will he plead against me with his great power? No; but he would put strength in me. There the righteous might dispute with him; so should I be delivered for ever from my judge. Behold, I go forward, but he is not there; and backward, but I cannot perceive him (Job 23:1-8 KJV). My foot hath held his steps, his way have I kept, and not declined. Neither have I gone back from the commandment of his lips; I have esteemed the words of his mouth more than my necessary food. But he is in one mind, and who can turn him? and what his soul desireth, even that he doeth. For he performeth the thing that is appointed for me: and many such things are with him (Job 23:11-14 KJV).

But he knoweth the way that I take: when he hath tried me, I shall come forth as gold (Job 23:10 KJV). For the eyes of the LORD run to and fro throughout the whole earth, to shew himself strong in the behalf of them whose heart is perfect toward him. Herein thou hast done foolishly: therefore from henceforth thou shalt have wars (2 Chronicles 16:9 KJV). Behold, God is mighty, and despiseth not any: he is mighty in strength and wisdom. He preserveth not the life of the wicked: but giveth right to the poor. He withdraweth not his eyes from the righteous: but with kings are they on the throne; yea, he doth establish them for ever, and they are exalted (Job 36:5-7 KJV). Therefore am I troubled at his presence: when I consider, I am afraid of him. For God maketh my heart soft, and the Almighty troubleth me: Because I was not cut off before the darkness, neither hath he covered the darkness from my face (Job 23:15-17 KJV)." The works of the LORD are great, sought out of all them that have pleasure therein (Psalm 111:2 KJV).

Undesirable Discipline

I was denied some desires, all because I loved Him more.
While they were after building buildings, I was on the threshing floor.

If I told you who they were, it would come as a surprise.
There is no need to point a finger, I scattereth with my eyes.

Reference: Proverbs 20:8 KJV

I delighted in the Lord, and He handed me desires.
He had me walking out His truths, but the "body" called them liars.

The discipline was not desired, but I was chosen and thus "gifted."
I almost hated His instructions but was surprised by what uplifted.

They're cut off from a trouble, and you could call it circumcision.
As many as desire as such deceived through circumvention.

They brag about evil desires; they praise the greedy while cursing God.
These are those who're of the body, but not the ones who're for the odds.

Some saints are known to speak in tongues. Who would dare to call them wicked?
They would say that they're the righteous. There's no discipline; they are wicked!

Undesirable Discipline

And though they say, The LORD liveth; surely they swear falsely. O LORD, are not thine eyes upon the truth? thou hast stricken them, but they have not grieved; thou hast consumed them, but they have refused to receive correction: they have made their faces harder than a rock; they have refused to return. Therefore I said, Surely these are poor; they are foolish: for they know not the way of the LORD, nor the judgment of their God. I will get me unto the great men, and will speak unto them; for they have known the way of the LORD, and the judgment of their God: but these have altogether broken the yoke, and burst the bonds (Jeremiah 5:2-5 KJV). For the house of Israel and the house of Judah have dealt very treacherously against me, saith the LORD. They have belied the LORD, and said, It is not he; neither shall evil come upon us; neither shall we see sword nor famine: (Jeremiah 5:11-12 KJV)!

Blessed is the man whom thou chastenest, O LORD, and teachest him out of thy law; That thou mayest give him rest from the days of adversity, until the pit be digged for the wicked. Shall the throne of iniquity have fellowship with thee, which frameth mischief by a law (Psalm 94:12-13, 20 KJV)? But these speak evil of those things which they know not: but what they know naturally, as brute beasts, in those things they corrupt themselves. Woe unto them! for they have gone in the way of Cain, and ran greedily after the error of Balaam for reward, and perished in the gainsaying of Core (Jude 1:10-11 KJV).

For the wicked boasteth of his heart's desire, and blesseth the covetous, whom the LORD abhorreth. The wicked, through the pride of his countenance, will not seek after God: God is not in all his thoughts. His ways are always grievous; thy judgments are far above out of his sight: as for all his enemies, he puffeth at them. He hath said in his heart, I shall not be moved: for I shall never be in adversity. His mouth is full of cursing and deceit and fraud: under his tongue is mischief and vanity (Psalm 10:3-7 KJV).

Insecure Discernment

Insecure discernment almost had me begging bread.
I was hungry for a pleasure that had almost left me dead.

The offer was so touching! You could say I had a feeling!
He led me to a certain path, but secret sins were more appealing.

I had an inkling of a sort. I sorted out my anxious thoughts.
I prayed about the matter, but the substance came to naught.

I acted out an answer, but I questioned the results.
Not in a disrespectful manner, making mockery insults.

Sometimes there's more than one experience written in a skillful song.
I shortened up the message and denied that which I long.

If I'm longing for right now, what would happen if I quit?
I cannot know the second, but this minute I am split.

I am not double-minded. What's a double ornate sword?
I've decorated wording that adulation can't afford.

Insecure about discernment; discerning when to meet with danger.
Wisdom always knew the truth, yet never left her looking stranger.

Insecure Discernment

Woe unto him that giveth his neighbour drink, that puttest thy bottle to him, and makest him drunken also, that thou mayest look on their nakedness! Thou art filled with shame for glory: drink thou also, and let thy foreskin be uncovered: the cup of the LORD's right hand shall be turned unto thee, and shameful spewing shall be on thy glory (Habakkuk 2:15-16 KJV). And I will bring the blind by a way that they knew not; I will lead them in paths that they have not known: I will make darkness light before them, and crooked things straight. These things will I do unto them, and not forsake them (Isaiah 42:16 KJV). And the parched ground shall become a pool, and the thirsty land springs of water: in the habitation of dragons, where each lay, shall be grass with reeds and rushes. And an highway shall be there, and a way, and it shall be called The way of holiness; the unclean shall not pass over it; but it shall be for those: the wayfaring men, though fools, shall not err therein (Isaiah 35:7-8 KJV).

No lion shall be there, nor any ravenous beast shall go up thereon, it shall not be found there; but the redeemed shall walk there: And the ransomed of the LORD shall return, and come to Zion with songs and everlasting joy upon their heads: they shall obtain joy and gladness, and sorrow and sighing shall flee away (Isaiah 35:9-10 KJV). I wisdom dwell with prudence, and find out knowledge of witty inventions (Proverbs 8:12 KJV). She is a tree of life to them that lay hold upon her: and happy is every one that retaineth her (Proverbs 3:18 KJV). …Who told thee that thou wast naked? Hast thou eaten of the tree, whereof I commanded thee that thou shouldest not eat (Genesis 3:11 KJV)?" They cause him to go naked without clothing, and they take away the sheaf from the hungry (Job 24:10 KJV). I have been young, and now am old; yet have I not seen the righteous forsaken, nor his seed begging bread (Psalm 37:25 KJV).

Who Told You?

Who told you that you were naked? Who told you that you were right?
Who told you to make more unpleasing offers in His sight?

There are some that you call friends, but God may say they're calloused climbers.
They never seek His godly wisdom, so they don't know His godly timers.

I waged war against a wisdom, but I failed to pass out food.
There was thirst for wisdom; the taste of mine could pass for rude.

Even with my godly wisdom, I lacked a gentle tongue.
Discernment hadn't surface. You could say that I was young.

Sometimes you'll need a sharper tongue, one that doesn't speak as tender,
Depending on the people, or the person, or the vendor.

The age may also matter. Just remember, don't think less.
He may reprimand your questioning and put your answer to the test.

He told me of my sins, in which I didn't know were there.
What He doesn't say out loud, He whispers in your ear to share.

Reference: Matthew 10:27 KJV

If you share that you're not a sinner, your heart's not where truth's at.
I'll meet you in your darkness and plainly ask, *Who told you that*?

Who Told You?

Acquaint now thyself with him, and be at peace: thereby good shall come unto thee. Receive, I pray thee, the law from his mouth, and lay up his words in thine heart (Job 22:21-22 KJV). If a brother or sister be naked, and destitute of daily food, And one of you say unto them, Depart in peace, be ye warmed and filled; notwithstanding ye give them not those things which are needful to the body; what doth it profit? Even so faith, if it hath not works, is dead being alone. Yea, a man may say, Thou hast faith, and I have works: shew me thy faith without thy works, and I will shew thee my faith by my works. Thou believest that there is one God; thou doest well: the devils also believe, and tremble. But wilt thou know. O vain man, that faith without works is dead (James 2:15-20 KJV)?

For thou hast taken a pledge from thy brother for nought, and stripped the naked of their clothing. Thou hast not given water to the weary to drink, and thou hast withholden bread from the hungry. But as for the mighty man, he had the earth; and the honourable man dwelt in it. Thou hast sent widows away empty, and the arms of the fatherless have been broken. Therefore snares are round about thee, and sudden fear troubleth thee; Or darkness, that thou canst not see; and abundance of waters cover thee (Job 22:6-11 KJV). Is not God in the height of heaven? and behold the height of the stars, how high they are! And thou sayest, How doth God know? can he judge through the dark cloud? Thick clouds are a covering to him, that he seeth not; and he walketh in the circuit of heaven. Hast thou marked the old way which wicked men have trodden? Which were cut down out of time, whose foundation was overflown with a flood: Which said unto God, Depart from us: and what can the Almighty do for them? Yet he filled their houses with good things: but the counsel of the wicked is far from me (Job 22:12-18 KJV).

The V-Card

Reference: Psalm 34:8 KJV

He said to taste and see but know sometimes the taste is nasty.
The V within the title; is it attributed to Vashti?

What kind of words of the transgressor doesn't appear as overthrown?
Abstract nouns had played their role and left messages unknown.

Worldly wisdom gives a meaning without submission of the soul.
But if a soul has been submitted, it achieves the higher goal.

His eyes have looked upon His person, and the method is concrete.
The knowledge of this truth is known as touchingly discreet.

These dense rain clouds are offensive. Who can handle such a teaching?
Am I losing offended brothers, or is it falsehood that I'm breaching?

You show yourself as pure; it's to the pure you call a bride.
Only few have touched its fragrance, so you let its knowledge hide.

What's strategically communicated? What's revealed can be alarming.
Because He's taking away authority, you can say that He's disarming.

What can the mind take away from these truths and these truths' densities?
They can add what He calls pure, with its alarming eccentricities.

The V-Card

Beware lest any man spoil you through philosophy and vain deceit, after the tradition of men, after the rudiments of the world, and not after Christ. For in him dwelleth all the fulness of the Godhead bodily. And ye are complete in him, which is the head of all principality and power: In whom also ye are circumcised with the circumcision made without hands, in putting off the body of the sins of the flesh by the circumcision of Christ: (Colossians 2:8-11 KJV). And you, being dead in your sins and the uncircumcision of your flesh, hath he quickened together with him, having forgiven you all trespasses; Blotting out the handwriting of ordinances that was against us, which was contrary to us, and took it out of the way, nailing it to his cross (Colossians 2:13-14 KJV).

Let no man therefore judge you in meat, or in drink, or in respect of an holyday, or of the new moon, or of the sabbath days: Which are a shadow of things to come; but the body is of Christ. Let no man beguile you of your reward in a voluntary humility and worshipping of angels, intruding into those things which he hath not seen, vainly puffed up by his fleshly mind, And not holding the Head, from which all the body by joints and bands having nourishment ministered, and knit together, increaseth with the increase of God. Wherefore if ye be dead with Christ from the rudiments of the world, why, as though living in the world, are ye subject to ordinances, (Touch not; taste not; handle not; Which all are to perish with the using;) after the commandments and doctrines of men? Which things have indeed a shew of wisdom in will worship, and humility, and neglecting of the body: not in any honour to the satisfying of the flesh (Colossians 2:16-23 KJV). Behold, I was shapen in iniquity; and in sin did my mother conceive me. Behold, thou desirest truth in the inward parts: and in the hidden part thou shalt make me to know wisdom (Psalm 51:5-6 KJV).

Bedroom Eyes

I speak of bedroom eyes, and it's because my eye be single.
I speak darkness and speak light; you could say that I'm bilingual.

Harlotry was fitting to the foolish, so she mothers.
They forbid the ones to marry who are the ones they call the *others*.

A covenant that is pure will always have a stormy season.
If you fail to keep the peace, there will be no bribe or reason.

The reason for their folly could be blamed on who denied.
What does a brainless expedition have on what their intellect defied?

Insecurities have a way of making light of what is dark.
The darkness then sheds light so that the temptress will outsmart.

What does smartness have on wisdom when His wisdom knows the game?
Is He playing on a weakness that will serve His holy name?

Hunger is no excuse for a beautiful thief to steal.
They're feeding an appetite, but they're still starving for a meal.

Should I think of sex as mammon when compared to His perfections?
I treasure all His answers and set my all on His affections.

Bedroom Eyes

The light of the body is the eye: if therefore thine eye be single, thy whole body shall be full of light. But if thine eye be evil, thy whole body shall be full of darkness. If therefore the light that is in thee be darkness, how great is that darkness (Matthew 6:20-22 KJV)! For by means of a whorish woman a man is brought to a piece of bread: and the adultress will hunt for the precious life. Can a man take fire in his bosom, and his clothes not be burned? Can one go upon hot coals, and his feet not be burned? So he that goeth in to his neighbour's wife; whosoever toucheth her shall not be innocent. Men do not despise a thief, if he steal to satisfy his soul when he is hungry; But if he be found, he shall restore sevenfold; he shall give all the substance of his house. But whoso committeth adultery with a woman lacketh understanding: he that doeth it destroyeth his own soul. A wound and dishonour shall he get; and his reproach shall not be wiped away (Proverbs 6:26-33 KJV).

Who is this that cometh up from the wilderness, leaning upon her beloved? I raised thee up under the apple tree: there thy mother brought thee forth: there she brought thee forth that bare thee. Set me as a seal upon thine heart, as a seal upon thine arm: for love is strong as death; jealousy is cruel as the grave: the coals thereof are coals of fire, which hath a most vehement flame. Many waters cannot quench love, neither can the floods drown it: if a man would give all the substance of his house for love, it would utterly be contemned (Songs of Songs 8:5-7 KJV). How is the faithful city become an harlot! it was full of judgment; righteousness lodged in it; but now murderers. Thy silver is become dross, thy wine mixed with water (Isaiah 1:21-22 KJV). Therefore thus saith the Lord GOD; Because ye are all become dross, behold, therefore I will gather you into the midst of Jerusalem. As they gather silver, and brass, and iron, and lead, and tin, into the midst of the furnace, to blow the fire upon it, to melt it; so will I gather you in mine anger and in my fury, and I will leave you there, and melt you. Yea, I will gather you, and blow upon you in the fire of my wrath, and ye shall be melted in the midst therof. As silver is melted in the midst of the furnace, so shall ye be melted in the midst thereof; and ye shall know that I the LORD have poured out my fury upon you (Ezekiel 22:19-22 KJV)."

"Sex" and Religion

Who are all these people saying the woman can't pursue?
Religion has a hold, and so their minds will not renew.

Religion tries to steal the truth from what we know as sex and "sex."
There's a purity undermined, if you don't mind if I perplex.

Certain males have dominated and demeaned the proper noun.
Improper dispositions divulged of victory till now.

The curse from the beginning has affected how one hears.
The double standard displays wisdom of who or what he's known to fear.

If wisdom is to her as wicked woman is to him,
These are they who know my truth and distinguish they from them.

He outsmarted what was worded to see who would learn the vow.
Two minds cannot partake with what one will or won't allow.

If you allow Him to expose you to your hidden fears and sins,
You will find that you're now last and where He humbles you begins.

Religion cannot sentence life within a death that is this pure.
They try to hide themselves from sin. What they call faith in not for sure.

"Sex" and Religion

O that thou wert as my brother, that sucked the breasts of my mother! when I should find thee without, I would kiss thee; yea, I should not be despised. I would lead thee, and bring thee into my mother's house, who would instruct me: I would cause thee to drink of spiced wine of the juice of my pomegranate (Song of Solomon 8:1-2 KJV). And the roof of thy mouth like the best wine for my beloved, that goeth down sweetly, causing the lips of those that are asleep to speak. I am my beloved's, and his desire is toward me (Song of Solomon 7:9-10 KJV). Wisdom hath builded her house, she hath hewn out her seven pillars: She hath killed her beasts; she hath mingled her wine; she hath also furnished her table (Proverbs 9:1-2 KJV). Come, eat of my bread, and drink of the wine which I have mingled (Proverbs 9:5 KJV).

How is the faithful city become an harlot! it was full of judgment; righteousness lodged in it; but now murderers. Thy silver is become dross, thy wine mixed with water: Thy princes are rebellious, and companions of thieves: every one loveth gifts, and followeth after rewards: they judge not the fatherless, neither doth the cause of the widow come unto them. Therefore saith the LORD, the LORD of hosts, the mighty One of Israel, Ah, I will ease me of mine adversaries, and avenge me of mine enemies: (Isaiah 1:21-24 KJV). And I will turn my hand upon thee, and purely purge away thy dross, and take away all thy tin: And I will restore thy judges as at the first, and thy counsellors as at the beginning: afterward thou shalt be called, The city of righteousness, the faithful city (Isaiah 1:25-26 KJV). Zion shall be redeemed with judgment, and her converts with righteousness. And the destruction of the transgressors and of the sinners shall be together, and they that forsake the LORD shall be consumed (Isaiah 1:27-28 KJV).

Temporary Pleasures

Why does flattery feel so good when you know their lips are lying?
Although I felt temptations, wisdom knew my flesh was dying.

Who knew that I had needs to which that fawning tongue had aimed?
Even though I did not sin, with my temptations, I felt shame.

The person using flattery can come to believe what they had felt.
They ~~pray~~ prey against at certain will, so with mockery they knelt.

I could speak more so on pain, but the process would be vivid.
The pain of patience I endured had me feeling somewhat livid.

My heart was overwhelmed while losing temporary treasures.
Right now, I serve the noun of how a timely process measures.

What is a momentary feeling, powerless to make a move?
It's a moving, meager meltdown, slipping in an open groove.

What you need is more eternal, so what's fitting is to sound.
I'm sounding the alarm, but certain pleasures have you bound.

Temporary Pleasures

Who can understand his errors? cleanse thou me from secret faults (Psalm 19:12 KJV). Behold, the days come, saith the LORD, that I will punish all them which are circumcised with the uncircumcised (Jeremiah 9:25 KJV). Thus saith the LORD, Let not the wise man glory in his wisdom, neither let the mighty man glory in his might, let not the rich man glory in his riches: But let him that glorieth glory in this, that he understandeth and knoweth me, that I am the LORD which exercise lovingkindness, judgment, and righteousness, in the earth: for in these things I delight, saith the LORD (Jeremiah 9:23-24 KJV).

Therefore hear now this, thou that art given to pleasures, that dwellest carelessly, that sayest in thine heart, I am, and none else beside me; I shall not sit as a widow, neither shall I know the loss of children (Isaiah 47:8 KJV). Woe unto them that call evil good, and good evil; that put darkness for light, and light for darkness; that put bitter for sweet, and sweet for bitter! Woe unto them that are wise in their own eyes, and prudent in their own sight! Woe unto them that are mighty to drink wine, and men of strength to mingle strong drink: Which justify the wicked for reward, and take away the righteousness of the righteous from him! (Isaiah 5:20-23 KJV). For thou hast trusted in thy wickedness: thou hast said, None seeth me. Thy wisdom and thy knowledge, it hath perverted thee; and thou hast said in thine heart, I am, and none else beside me (Isaiah 47:10 KJV). Therefore shall evil come upon thee; thou shalt not know from whence it riseth: and mischief shall fall upon thee; thou shalt not be able to put it off: and desolation shall come upon thee suddenly, which thou shalt not know (Isaiah 47:11 KJV).

Come Up Hither

Can you hear the worded gesture, because I'm known to speak with archness?
I shout aloud his hidden truths that are meant to deafen treasured darkness.

I'm writing in a way to help you understand the knave.
What's becoming of a method without the man that's there to save?

They think that they're so giving, but they don't understand their seeds.
They boast about their power, but they don't understand their needs.

What is it about the water in correlation to the blood?
The blood released a seed and the seed sank into mud.

Do not miss this point on how some frozen vessels trickle.
They parade around His truths and so their leadership is fickle.

A dime a dozen saint is what I call a pond that nickels.
A quarter of a river is what I call a truth that tickles

The land they think they own has produced its thorns and thistles.
I'm brushing up on truth, and so, I work against the bristle.

Come Up Hither

The righteous perisheth, and no man layeth it to heart: and merciful men are taken away, none considering that the righteous is taken away from the evil to come. He shall enter into peace: they shall rest in their beds, each one walking in his uprightness. But draw near hither, ye sons of the sorceress, the seed of the adulterer and the whore. Against whom do ye sport yourselves? Against whom make ye a wide mouth, and draw out the tongue? Are ye not children of transgression, a seed of falsehood (Isaiah 57:1-4 KJV). Upon a lofty and high mountain hast thou set thy bed: even thither wentest thou up to offer sacrifice. Behind the doors also and the posts hast thou set up thy remembrance: for thou hast discovered thyself to another than me, and art gone up; thou hast enlarged thy bed, and made thee a covenant with them; thou lovedst their bed where thou sawest it (Isaiah 57:7-8 KJV).

And thou wentest to the king with ointment, and didst increase thy perfumes, and didst send thy messengers far off, and didst debase thyself even unto hell. Thou art wearied in the greatness of thy way; yet saidst thou not, There is no hope: thou hast found the life of thine hand; therefore thou wast not grieved. And of whom hast thou been afraid or feared, that thou hast lied, and hast not remembered me, nor laid it to thy heart? have not I held my peace even of old, and thou fearest me not? I will declare thy righteousness, and thy works; for they shall not profit thee. When thou criest, let thy companies deliver thee; but the wind shall carry them all away; vanity shall take them: but he that putteth his trust in me shall possess the land, and shall inherit my holy mountain (Isaiah 57:9-13 KJV).

Your Worst Nightmare

What is your worst nightmare, but a fantasy fulfilled.
You thought it was a need, but it was the "wanting" that had killed.

Overnight successes have a way of disappointing.
They gained material wealth, but they rejected the anointing.

A wealth of pleasure only means that your fun is transitory.
The funny thing about His justice makes His judgment mandatory.

What do you call its growth if the seed won't fall and die?
You can call it what you want, but I'll call the look a lie.

Some say they hear His voice, but they'll hear "depart from Me."
Graven images have their facades, but that's all they'll ever be.

They speak without an understanding and with sheer vituperation.
Because they acted before answered, they will be met with trepidation.

I'm questioning the men. When did the noun become possessive?
I'm now hinting at a truth and kind of love that's more reflective.

If your strength is in a power, what kind of common noun is he?
My weakness is uncommon as it now relates to she.

Your Worst Nightmare

Surely men of low degree are vanity, and men of high degree are a lie: to be laid in the balance, they are altogether lighter than vanity (Psalm 62:9 KJV). Now go, write it before them in a table, and note it in a book, that it may be for the time to come for ever and ever: That this is a rebellious people, lying children, children that will not hear the law of the LORD (Isaiah 30:8-9 KJV). For out of the heart proceed evil thoughts, murders, adulteries, fornications, thefts, false witness, blasphemies (Matthew 15:19 KJV). Behold, the name of the LORD cometh from far, burning with his anger, and the burden thereof is heavy: his lips are full of indignation, and his tongue as a devouring fire: And his breath, as an overflowing stream, shall reach to the midst of the neck, to sift the nations with the sieve of vanity: and there shall be a bridle in the jaws of the people, causing them to err (Isaiah 30:27-28 KJV). And the LORD shall cause his glorious voice to be heard, and shall shew the lighting down of his arm, with the indignation of his anger, and with the flame of a devouring fire, with scattering, and tempest, and hailstones (Isaiah 30:30 KJV). For through the voice of the LORD shall the Assyrian be beaten down, which smote with a rod (Isaiah 30:31 KJV).

Woe to the rebellious children, saith the LORD, that take counsel, but not of me; and that cover with a covering, but not of my Spirit, that they may add sin to sin: That walk to go down into Egypt, and have not asked at my mouth; to strengthen themselves in the strength of Pharaoh, and to trust in the shadow of Egypt! Therefore shall the strength of Pharaoh be your shame, and the shadow of Egypt your confusion. For his princes were at Zoan, and his ambassadors came to Hanes. They were all ashamed of a people that could not profit them, nor be an help nor profit, but a shame, and also a reproach. The burden of the beasts of the south: into the land of trouble and anguish, from whence come the young and old lion, the viper and fiery flying serpent, they will carry their riches upon the shoulders of young asses, and their treasures upon the bunches of camels, to a people that shall not profit them (Isaiah 30:1-6 KJV).

What's the Challenge?

The challenge is to love, and I speak the task with favor.
What is hateful serves the sentence in a law to love thy neighbor.

If the challenge is to sanction as the taking is to give.
The motive is to measure as the method is to sieve.

There's a balancing technique. Learn to take and thus receive.
Only to the thriving soul that this command would cause to grieve.

Denying one's affluence would be to understand the need.
Parting with a reputation would be to understand the reed.

If wisdom is as wisdom does and the harvest is of plenty,
Study the matter thus again; within the lines seeing twenty-twenty.

What's the challenge is the question, yet the answer is the sinker.
Every line is taking action, but only given to the thinker.

As I served my neighbor, I saw what once was unforeseen.
He can expose you to yourself if you should challenge what I mean.

It's challenging to choose the narrow path or narrow pit.
Just as it's challenging to know just when I stand or when I sit.

What's the Challenge?

Better is a dinner of herbs where love is, than a stalled ox and hatred therewith (Proverbs 15:17 KJV). Behold, the eyes of the Lord GOD are upon the sinful kingdom, and I will destroy it from off the face of the earth; saving that I will not utterly destroy the house of Jacob, saith the LORD. For, lo, I will command, and I will sift the house of Israel among all nations, like as corn is sifted in a sieve, yet shall not the least grain fall upon the earth. All the sinners of my people shall die by the sword, which say, The evil shall not overtake nor prevent us (Amos 9:8-10 KJV). For now they shall say, We have no king, because we feared not the LORD; what then should a king do to us? They have spoken words, swearing falsely in making a covenant: thus judgment springeth up as hemlock in the furrows of the field (Hosea 10:3-4 KJV).

Israel is an empty vine, he bringeth forth fruit unto himself: according to the multitude of his fruit he hath increased the altars; according to the goodness of his land they have made goodly images (Hosea 10:1 KJV). Israel is an empty vine, he bringeth forth fruit unto himself: according to the multitude of his fruit he hath increased the altars; according to the goodness of his land they have made goodly images (Hosea 10:1-2 KJV). It is in my desire that I should chastise them; and the people shall be gathered against them, when they shall bind themselves in their two furrows. And Ephraim is as an heifer that is taught, and loveth to tread out the corn; but I passed over upon her fair neck: I will make Ephraim to ride; Judah shall plow, and Jacob shall break his clods. Sow to yourselves in righteousness, reap in mercy; break up your fallow ground: for it is time to seek the LORD, till he come and rain righteousness upon you. Ye have plowed wickedness, ye have reaped iniquity; ye have eaten the fruit of lies: because thou didst trust in thy way, in the multitude of thy mighty men (Hosea 10:10-13 KJV).

Love Thy Neighbor

Their cleanliness was "spotted" by successes so one loathes.
The woman who's called wisdom, naked's truth and so she clothes.

They are known to wear my clothing, but these wolves cannot outdress.
They took with worldly grasping that left them trying to impress.

I'm loving on the truth, and you could say I'm blowing whistles.
I'm calling out what's false and watching them pick their fruit from thistles.

They were told the truth, but the truth did not take root.
They put the cash ~~word~~ to work, but they produced an evil fruit.

Cash is not the focal word, but it's with "word" it interchanges.
My intellect is not your choice; it can't be bought and so it stranges.

In other words, my tongue is lit with strangest literary flair.
You could learn to kiss the donkey and love your neighbor if you dare.

Love Thy Neighbor

Take ye heed every one of his neighbour, and trust ye not in any brother: for every brother will utterly supplant, and every neighbour will walk with slanders. And they will deceive every one his neighbour, and will not speak the truth: they have taught their tongue to speak lies, and weary themselves to commit iniquity. Thine habitation is in the midst of deceit; through deceit they refuse to know me, saith the LORD. Their tongue is as an arrow shot out; it speaketh deceit: one speaketh peaceably to his neighbour with his mouth, but in heart he layeth his wait. Shall I not visit them for these things? saith the LORD: shall not my soul be avenged on such a nation as this (Jeremiah 9:4-6, 8-9 KJV)?

Now also many nations are gathered against thee, that say, Let her be defiled, and let our eye look upon Zion. But they know not the thoughts of the LORD, neither understand they his counsel: for he shall gather them as the sheaves into the floor (Micah 4:11-12 KJV). Whose fan is in his hand, and he will throughly purge his floor, and gather his wheat into the garner; but he will burn up the chaff with unquenchable fire (Matthew 3:12 KJV)." Israel is swallowed up: now shall they be among the Gentiles as a vessel wherein is no pleasure. For they are gone up to Assyria, a wild ass alone by himself: Ephraim hath hired lovers. Yea, though they have hired among the nations, now will I gather them, and they shall sorrow a little for the burden of the king of princes (Hosea 8:8-10 KJV). Because Ephraim hath made many altars to sin, altars shall be unto him to sin. I have written to him the great things of my law, but they were counted as a strange thing (Hosea 8:11-12 KJV). For he knoweth vain men: he seeth wickedness also; will he not then consider it? For vain men would be wise, though man be born like a wild ass's colt (Job 11:11-12 KJV).

A.I.R Conditioned
Agape's Illicit Responsiveness

A love that is of lust will not accept how love responded.
There's a love that's in your heart, but it's a love that is despondent.

What is illicit is not hidden, so that the loving gesture flaunts.
It parades around a truth, so it's the truth that the lie taunts.

A love born of rejection paved the way to being conditioned.
Its path paramount to changing so that your love is repositioned.

I had a team of opposition. My zeal was known as ardent.
Although I heard one's scoffing. I might say one touched my garment.

Insight: Ezekiel 44:19 KJV

The arrogant claimed I bit her hand. She hit me with contempt.
If her love was called agape, it was this love that was exempt.

If the handout was to feed as the scriptures are to food,
Who's sitting at a table, and yet the ones that He excludes?

Who puffeth up at truth? What is a love without longevity?
My times are in His hands. What is life without His brevity?

A.I.R. Conditioned

I have loved you with an everlasting love; I have drawn you with unfailing kindness (Jeremiah 31:3 KJV). Hear the word of the LORD, you nations; proclaim it in distant coastlands: 'He who scattered Israel will gather them and will watch over his flock like a shepherd.' For the LORD will deliver Jacob and redeem them from the hand of those stronger than they (Jeremiah 31:10-11 KJV). Draw me, we will run after thee: the king hath brought me into his chambers: we will be glad and rejoice in thee, we will remember thy love more than wine: the upright love thee (Song of Solomon 1:4 KJV). I charge you, O ye daughters of Jerusalem, by the roes, and by the hinds of the field, that ye stir not up, nor awake my love, till he please (Song of Solomon 2:7 KJV). They have corrupted themselves, their spot is not the spot of his children: they are a perverse and crooked generation (Deuteronomy 32:5 KJV).

But God is the judge: he putteth down one, and setteth up another. For in the hand of the LORD there is a cup, and the wine is red; it is full of mixture; and he poureth out of the same: but the dregs thereof, all the wicked of the earth shall wring them out, and drink them (Psalm 75:7-8 KJV). Wisdom hath builded her house, she hath hewn out her seven pillars: She hath killed her beasts; she hath mingled her wine; she hath also furnished her table. She hath sent forth her maidens: she crieth upon the highest places of the city, Whoso is simple, let him turn in hither: as for him that wanteth understanding, she saith to him, Come, eat of my bread, and drink of the wine which I have mingled. Forsake the foolish, and live; and go in the way of understanding (Proverbs 9:1-6 KJV)." When I shall receive the congregation I will judge uprightly. The earth and all the inhabitants thereof are dissolved: I bear up the pillars of it. Selah (Psalm 75:2-3 KJV). All the horns of the wicked also will I cut off; but the horns of the righteous shall be exalted (Psalm 75:10 KJV).

Fruit of the Spirit: **Faith**

Psalm 56:1 KJV

Be merciful unto me, O God: for man would swallow me up; he fighting daily oppresseth me.

A Kind of Kindness

There's a kindness that can blind you. There's a kindness that can kill.
A kind of kindness kissing death made learning righteousness a thrill.

This kind of kindness had me baffled. I didn't see it coming.
He exposed me to my secrets. The human heart and mind are cunning.

Reference: Psalm 64:6 NIV

What I thought was wisdom would be failure at its worst.
He had given me new wine. I almost made the wineskins burst.

I thought I could not stand. I thought that I would fall.
I knew my own temptations. I needed knowledge for them all.

He said, "Don't run from where I send you. Go ahead and let it be."
He had me questioning technique; and so, what does He mean by flee?

What does His kindness mean, when the wind sounds more like trouble?
If He should name the drink He mixed, He'd call it mercy on the double.

A Kind of Kindness

He that hateth dissembleth with his lips, and layeth up deceit within him; When he speaketh fair, believe him not: for there are seven abominations in his heart. Whose hatred is covered by deceit, his wickedness shall be shewed before the whole congregation (Proverbs 26:24-26 KJV). In thee, O LORD, do I put my trust; let me never be ashamed: deliver me in thy righteousness. Bow down thine ear to me; deliver me speedily: be thou my strong rock, for an house of defence to save me. For thou art my rock and my fortress; therefore for thy name's sake lead me, and guide me. Pull me out of the net that they have laid privily for me: for thou art my strength. Into thine hand I commit my spirit: thou hast redeemed me, O LORD God of truth (Psalm 31:1-5 KJV). The rich man's wealth is his strong city, and as an high wall in his own conceit (Proverbs 18:11 KJV).

But I trusted in thee, O LORD: I said, Thou art my God. My times are in thy hand: deliver me from the hand of mine enemies, and from them that persecute me. Make thy face to shine upon thy servant: save me for thy mercies' sake. Let me not be ashamed, O LORD; for I have called upon thee: let the wicked be ashamed, and let them be silent in the grave. Let the lying lips be put to silence; which speak grievous things proudly and contemptuously against the righteous. Oh how great is thy goodness, which thou hast laid up for them that fear thee; which thou hast wrought for them that trust in thee before the sons of men! Thou shalt hide them in the secret of thy presence from the pride of man: thou shalt keep them secretly in a pavilion from the strife of tongues. Blessed be the LORD: for he hath shewed me his marvellous kindness in a strong city. For I said in my haste, I am cut off from before thine eyes: nevertheless thou heardest the voice of my supplications when I cried unto thee. O love the LORD, all ye his saints: for the LORD preserveth the faithful, and plentifully rewardeth the proud doer. Be of good courage, and he shall strengthen your heart, all ye that hope in the LORD (Psalm 31:14-24 KJV).

Usury

Why should some folks do the lending to someone who can't repay?
Cross one's hands; reverse the problem; it'll show the answer. Hit replay.

If they could bet their hand on giving, they'd lose kindness on a dime.
If time compared to logs, who'd move one splinter at a time?

Time has changed the denotation; go back to the original meaning.
Interest is as interest serves; which discerns the time of gleaning?

Someone spoke with loving words, but within was inner baseness.
The first had did his pleading until the second made it caseless.

To think the one who knew you; would be the one you call pretender.
I heard the outside voice; and you gave props to the contender.

I never would have thought. You said he sought his own desire.
He parted from a soundness that called his noisiness a liar.

What he said was spoken softly but applied to certain servants.
The truth of it works patience. Patience's dying, so it urgents.

The tongue has met the lips. They are challenged to a duel.
Their words were formed together, so which ~~won~~ one had played the fool?

Usury

He that is first in his own cause seemeth just; but his neighbour cometh and searcheth him. The lot causeth contentions to cease, and parteth between the mighty (Proverbs 18:17-18 KJV). The poor and the deceitful man meet together: the LORD lighteneth both their eyes (Proverbs 29:13 KJV). Therefore when thou doest thine alms, do not sound a trumpet before thee, as the hypocrites do in the synagogues and in the streets, that they may have glory of men. Verily I say unto you, They have their reward. But when thou doest alms, let not thy left hand know what thy right hand doeth: (Matthew 6:2-3 KJV).

When the Son of man shall come in his glory, and all the holy angels with him, then shall he sit upon the throne of his glory: And before him shall be gathered all nations: and he shall separate them one from another, as a shepherd divideth his sheep from the goats: And he shall set the sheep on his right hand, but the goats on the left. Then shall the King say unto them on his right hand, Come, ye blessed of my Father, inherit the kingdom prepared for you from the foundation of the world: For I was an hungred, and ye gave me meat: I was thirsty, and ye gave me drink: I was a stranger, and ye took me in: Naked, and ye clothed me: I was sick, and ye visited me: I was in prison, and ye came unto me (Matthew 25:31-36 KJV). But love ye your enemies, and do good, and lend, hoping for nothing again; and your reward shall be great, and ye shall be the children of the Highest: for he is kind unto the unthankful and to the evil (Luke 6:35 KJV). The desire of the righteous is only good: but the expectation of the wicked is wrath. There is that scattereth, and yet increaseth; and there is that withholdeth more than is meet, but it tendeth to poverty (Proverbs 11:23-24 KJV).

Taxed!

Both good and evil are promiscuously scattered.
All nature mirrored by human nature is shattered.

I was looking for an answer, but I didn't know the question.
He had given me the answer; what's to question is the question.

Total darkness for the wicked, who think they know the way.
They're flummoxed at freewheeling, yet due process paved the way.

If their light is actually darkness, do I snuff out a flickering candle?
The tariffs waged a pretty penny at a price they couldn't handle.

I'm writing to inform you that there has been an underpayment.
My feet went down a path that you could call mosaic pavement.

Take a step, then go and file. *Request for reconsideration?*
I'll give you time, but your feet are set for fixed obliteration.

You can double-check your records, but I'm known to cross-examine.
The trail has left a question. Who's trained to hear Me through the famine?

I can assure you; your insurance claims will therefore be denied.
They dodged a certain policy, but it was Promise they defied.

Can you answer a quick question? What is a faulty claim that maxed?
Since I know how you will answer, then I guess I'll leave you TAXED!

Taxed

Rest in the LORD, and wait patiently for him: fret not thyself because of him who prospereth in his way, because of the man who bringeth wicked devices to pass. Cease from anger, and forsake wrath: fret not thyself in any wise to do evil. For evildoers shall be cut off: but those that wait upon the LORD, they shall inherit the earth. For yet a little while, and the wicked shall not be: yea, thou shalt diligently consider his place, and it shall not be. But the meek shall inherit the earth; and shall delight themselves in the abundance of peace. The wicked plotteth against the just, and gnasheth upon him with his teeth. The LORD shall laugh at him: for he seeth that his day is coming. The wicked have drawn out the sword, and have bent their bow, to cast down the poor and needy, and to slay such as be of upright conversation. Their sword shall enter into their own heart, and their bows shall be broken (Psalm 37:7-15 KJV).

A little that a righteous man hath is better than the riches of many wicked. For the arms of the wicked shall be broken: but the LORD upholdeth the righteous. The LORD knoweth the days of the upright: and their inheritance shall be for ever. They shall not be ashamed in the evil time: and in the days of famine they shall be satisfied (Psalm 37:16-19 KJV). Rejoice in the LORD, O ye righteous: for praise is comely for the upright (Psalm 33:1 KJV). For the word of the LORD is right; and all his works are done in truth. He loveth righteousness and judgment: the earth is full of the goodness of the LORD (Psalm 33:4-5 KJV). The LORD looked down from heaven upon the children of men, to see if there were any that did understand, and seek God (Psalm 14:2 KJV). By the word of the LORD were the heavens made; and all the host of them by the breath of his mouth. He gathereth the waters of the sea together as an heap: he layeth up the depth in storehouses. Let all the earth fear the LORD: let all the inhabitants of the world stand in awe of him. For he spake, and it was done; he commanded, and it stood fast (Psalm 33:6-9 KJV).

The Nth Degree

He said I had some power, but I didn't know I did.

If I had knowledge of the truth, I was hindered by what hid.

Who wants the path of life when it offers you less pleasure?

What He offers brings a darkness to expose the hidden treasure.

Nothing's adding up! A Yoke of ease has been subtracted.

The burden of the light has been as one that was redacted.

He denied my forward progress, but He said it was protective.

Who speaks the word of God so it translates as more invective?

His decisions had me weary. I couldn't see past my desires.

The one who often gets their way may be the one He calls denier.

I was told I "follow" wrong, and some would say that I'm dismissive.

My discernment of the matter made my answering permissive.

There comes a time when I think I'm right, and a time I know I'm wrong.

Corrective measures will be given; worldly treasures will prolong.

I'm growing right-on-time, despite the wrongness of my youth.

Their own knowledge misinformed them; therefore, cancelling a truth.

My expectations misinformed me of when and where and who I'd be.

My circumstances searched my heart and pointed to the Nth Degree.

The Nth Degree

The fear of the LORD is clean, enduring for ever: the judgments of the LORD are true and righteous altogether (Psalm 19:9 KJV). He shall have dominion also from sea to sea, and from the river unto the ends of the earth (Psalm 72:8 KJV). The kings of Tarshish and of the isles shall bring presents: the kings of Sheba and Seba shall offer gifts. Yea, all kings shall fall down before him: all nations shall serve him. For he shall deliver the needy when he crieth; the poor also, and him that hath no helper. He shall spare the poor and needy, and shall save the souls of the needy. He shall redeem their soul from deceit and violence: and precious shall their blood be in his sight. And he shall live, and to him shall be given of the gold of Sheba: prayer also shall be made for him continually; and daily shall he be praised. There shall be an handful of corn in the earth upon the top of the mountains; the fruit thereof shall shake like Lebanon: and they of the city shall flourish like grass of the earth (Psalm 72:10-16 KJV).

And men shall speak of the might of thy terrible acts: and I will declare thy greatness. They shall abundantly utter the memory of thy great goodness, and shall sing of thy righteousness. The LORD is gracious, and full of compassion; slow to anger, and of great mercy. The LORD is good to all: and his tender mercies are over all his works. All thy works shall praise thee, O LORD; and thy saints shall bless thee (Psalm 145:6-10 KJV). His name shall endure for ever: his name shall be continued as long as the sun: and men shall be blessed in him: all nations shall call him blessed. Blessed be the LORD God, the God of Israel, who only doeth wondrous things. And blessed be his glorious name for ever: and let the whole earth be filled with his glory; Amen, and Amen (Psalm 72:17-19 KJV)!

Talking Walls

I name this "Talking Walls." It's a spin-off of a phrase.
I'm eulogizing songs, which is a spin-off of a praise.

Some say, "If walls could talk," but I'm saying that they can.
They shout out all their secrets of a lust that one demands.

I heard them whisper of my weakness, saying my wants were truly simple.
I recognized a falsehood outside the walls and in the temple.

These walls exposed some truths; they revealed some secret faults.
True kings are warned by Wisdom's judgment, and he fears Him, so he halts.

The fear of the LORD is clean and enduring forevermore.
I'm speaking of a type of testing, yet I'm telling you the score.

The walls said, "No one's perfect." What I heard? "Convert your soul."
A vote between the sayings became the one that ruled the poll.

Their words have gone throughout the world; the walls have surely told.
They proclaim His glorious victories, which are messages of old.

Talking Walls

Behold, his soul which is lifted up is not upright in him: but the just shall live by his faith. Yea also, because he transgresseth by wine, he is a proud man, neither keepeth at home, who enlargeth his desire as hell, and is as death, and cannot be satisfied, but gathereth unto him all nations, and heapeth unto him all people: Shall not all these take up a parable against him, and a taunting proverb against him, and say, Woe to him that increaseth that which is not his! how long? and to him that ladeth himself with thick clay! Shall they not rise up suddenly that shall bite thee, and awake that shall vex thee, and thou shalt be for booties unto them? Because thou hast spoiled many nations, all the remnant of the people shall spoil thee; because of men's blood, and for the violence of the land, of the city, and of all that dwell therein (Habakkuk 2:4-8 KJV).

Woe to him that coveteth an evil covetousness to his house, that he may set his nest on high, that he may be delivered from the power of evil! Thou hast consulted shame to thy house by cutting off many people, and hast sinned against thy soul. For the stone shall cry out of the wall, and the beam out of the timber shall answer it. Woe to him that buildeth a town with blood, and stablisheth a city by iniquity! Behold, is it not of the LORD of hosts that the people shall labour in the very fire, and the people shall weary themselves for very vanity? For the earth shall be filled with the knowledge of the glory of the LORD, as the waters cover the sea (Habakkuk 2:9-14 KJV). And it shall come to pass in the day of the LORD's sacrifice, that I will punish the princes, and the king's children, and all such as are clothed with strange apparel (Zephaniah 1:8 KJV). Blessed is the man whom thou chastenest, O LORD, and teachest him out of thy law; That thou mayest give him rest from the days of adversity, until the pit be digged for the wicked (Psalm 94:12-13 KJV).

Reign!

Your rain fell on me.

Your Reign took control of me.

When I was down, Your Reign washed my sins away.

Your Reign is the same today.

When I was in despair,

Your reign replaced my tears and gave me a new breath of fresh air.

The LORD Reigns!

The rain falls on the unjust and the just.

The LORD Reigns, so we must.

Tell others that He Reigns!

When it rains, He pours,

On everything that's yours.

His rain falls and opens doors,

So, let the rain fall on me.

Let your Reign help me see,

That your blessings of allowing the rain to fall,

Will help me become and give my all,

So I know that when the rain falls,

It only makes me a better king.

Reign

The LORD liveth; and blessed be my rock; and let the God of my salvation be exalted. It is God that avengeth me, and subdueth the people under me. He delivereth me from mine enemies: yea, thou liftest me up above those that rise up against me: thou hast delivered me from the violent man. Therefore will I give thanks unto thee, O LORD, among the heathen, and sing praises unto thy name. Great deliverance giveth he to his king; and sheweth mercy to his anointed, to David, and to his seed for evermore (Psalm 18:46-50 KJV). Give the king thy judgments, O God, and thy righteousness unto the king's son. He shall judge thy people with righteousness, and thy poor with judgment. The mountains shall bring peace to the people, and the little hills, by righteousness. He shall judge the poor of the people, he shall save the children of the needy, and shall break in pieces the oppressor. They shall fear thee as long as the sun and moon endure, throughout all generations (Psalm 72:1-5 KJV)!

He shall come down like rain upon the mown grass: as showers that water the earth. In his days shall the righteous flourish; and abundance of peace so long as the moon endureth (Psalm 72:6-7 KJV). For by thee I have run through a troop; and by my God have I leaped over a wall. As for God, his way is perfect: the word of the LORD is tried: he is a buckler to all those that trust in him. For who is God save the LORD? or who is a rock save our God? It is God that girdeth me with strength, and maketh my way perfect. He maketh my feet like hinds' feet, and setteth me upon my high places. He teacheth my hands to war, so that a bow of steel is broken by mine arms. Thou hast also given me the shield of thy salvation: and thy right hand hath holden me up, and thy gentleness hath made me great. For thou hast girded me with strength unto the battle: thou hast subdued under me those that rose up against me. The LORD liveth; and blessed be my rock; and let the God of my salvation be exalted (Psalm 18:29-35, 39, 46 KJV)!

Feigned Words

How do you keep from speaking guile if you don't know you're being deceived?

If two words can contradict, who's to say what one received?

If I didn't know what's better, I would say the curse was kindness.

He didn't let them know the future. He let the liars keep their blindness.

Job 12:16 KJV

The deceived and the deceiver, He said, "Both of them are mine!"

There's a purpose to the mixture. The method has and will refine.

I was discerning when to stay and discerning when to leave.

Discerning when to shout for joy and also learning when to grieve.

Who grieved the Spirit by their words, therefore cancelling a truth?

Who dared to live and speak my word, representing godly couth?

I was rich, but was without, and surely so were they.

My richness was in speech and was without what was to say.

Psalm 62:3 KJV

They imagined mischief against one man. His answer was in numbers.

Their richness made them sleep. He counted out what made them slumber.

The richness of the Spirit's language kills the threat of what allures.

The "errors" of His ways denies the wealth of what assures.

Feigned Words

Blessed is the man whom thou chastenest, O LORD, and teachest him out of thy law; That thou mayest give him rest from the days of adversity, until the pit be digged for the wicked. For the LORD will not cast off his people, neither will he forsake his inheritance. But judgment shall return unto righteousness: and all the upright in heart shall follow it (Psalm 94:12-15 KJV). Hear this, all ye people; give ear, all ye inhabitants of the world: Both low and high, rich and poor, together. My mouth shall speak of wisdom; and the meditation of my heart shall be of understanding. I will incline mine ear to a parable: I will open my dark saying upon the harp. Wherefore should I fear in the days of evil, when the iniquity of my heels shall compass me about? They that trust in their wealth, and boast themselves in the multitude of their riches (Psalm 49:1-6 KJV).

For there is no faithfulness in their mouth; their inward part is very wickedness; their throat is an open sepulchre; they flatter with their tongue. Destroy thou them, O God; let them fall by their own counsels; cast them out in the multitude of their transgressions; for they have rebelled against thee (Psalm 5:9-10 KJV). This their way is their folly: yet their posterity approve their sayings. Selah. Like sheep they are laid in the grave; death shall feed on them; and the upright shall have dominion over them in the morning; and their beauty shall consume in the grave from their dwelling (Psalm 49:13-14 KJV). For then will I turn to the people a pure language, that they may all call upon the name of the LORD, to serve him with one consent (Zephaniah 3:9 KJV). Associate yourselves, O ye people, and ye shall be broken in pieces; and give ear, all ye of far countries: gird yourselves, and ye shall be broken in pieces; gird yourselves, and ye shall be broken in pieces. Take counsel together, and it shall come to nought; speak the word, and it shall not stand: for God is with us (Isaiah 8:9-10 KJV).

A Different Kind of Goodbye!

What can I say but thank you! What can I do but praise!
We came together, and we worshiped! We shared all those days!

Although my days with you were fewer; they were fewer than expected.
I was surrounded by my fears, and still I found myself protected.

Your kindness was to me as uncommon sound rebuttal.
It put His wisdom on display, that which was hidden and was subtle.

When I first would visit you, I was feeling kind of young.
This infrequent palate helps me understand this tongue.

He propositioned me to sit. I ate a certain kind of food.
I offer you a sense of taste, if you allow me to exude.

What is to question living answers? What is a word that's never clutched?
What is healing is to thank you, knowing that our lives didn't go untouched.

Our dining was a blessing! Thanks for all you've done!
This cannot be goodbye when different times have just begun!

A Different Kind of Goodbye

When I remember these things, I pour out my soul in me: for I had gone with the multitude, I went with them to the house of God, with the voice of joy and praise, with a multitude that kept holyday (Psalm 42:4 KJV)! We took sweet counsel together, and walked unto the house of God in company (Psalm 55:14 KJV). I hate, I despise your feast days, and I will not smell in your solemn assemblies. Though ye offer me burnt offerings and your meat offerings, I will not accept them: neither will I regard the peace offerings of your fat beasts. Take thou away from me the noise of thy songs; for I will not hear the melody of thy viols (Amos 5:21-23 KJV). Judge me, O LORD; for I have walked in mine integrity: I have trusted also in the LORD; therefore I shall not slide. Examine me, O LORD, and prove me; try my reins and my heart. For thy lovingkindness is before mine eyes: and I have walked in thy truth. I have not sat with vain persons, neither will I go in with dissemblers. I have hated the congregation of evil doers; and will not sit with the wicked. I will wash mine hands in innocency: so will I compass thine altar, O LORD: (Psalm 26:1-6 KJV).

~~That~~ I ~~may~~ publish with the voice of thanksgiving, and tell of all thy wondrous works (Psalm 26:7 KJV). But who may abide the day of his coming? and who shall stand when he appeareth? for he is like a refiner's fire, and like fullers' soap: And he shall sit as a refiner and purifier of silver: and he shall purify the sons of Levi, and purge them as gold and silver, that they may offer unto the LORD an offering in righteousness. Then shall the offering of Judah and Jerusalem be pleasant unto the LORD, as in the days of old, and as in former years (Malachi 3:2-4 KJV). In those days, and in that time, saith the LORD, the children of Israel shall come, they and the children of Judah together, going and weeping: they shall go, and seek the LORD their God. They shall ask the way to Zion with their faces thitherward, saying, Come, and let us join ourselves to the LORD in a perpetual covenant that shall not be forgotten (Jeremiah 50:4-5 KJV).

A Stranger's Voice?

I spoke His words with loving care, but they thought I was a stranger.
They're unfamiliar with a tone, which makes this proposition stranger.

I kissed a servant's cheek, and yet was not the common traitor.
The roles had been reversed, which serves the proper timing later.

Now's the time to take His offer. The gift of life remains the same.
If you take what death has offered, well, then whose life is there to blame?

They were strangers to His ways. They couldn't understand the call.
Yet they mock Him for His service, which is the product of the fall.

How can it be that one can learn and never come to know the truth?
It's like a child who grows, but never comes out of one's youth.

Romans 10:17 KJV
Faith cometh by hearing and hearing by the word of God.
Hear I Am's voice! Who'll feel I Am's rod?

Hear I Am's voice. Hear I Am's choice. Here I am so I rejoice.

He told me about the snare. He told me to care.
He told me to dare to say hear I Am's voice!

A Stranger's Voice?

…He calleth his own sheep by name, and leadeth them out. And when he putteth forth his own sheep, he goeth before them, and the sheep follow him: for they know his voice. And a stranger will they not follow, but will flee from him: for they know not the voice of strangers (John 10:3-5 KJV). For a whore is a deep ditch; and a strange woman is a narrow pit (Proverbs 23:27 KJV). Beware of false prophets, which come to you in sheep's clothing, but inwardly they are ravening wolves. Ye shall know them by their fruits. Do men gather grapes of thorns, or figs of thistles? Even so every good tree bringeth forth good fruit; but a corrupt tree bringeth forth evil fruit. A good tree cannot bring forth evil fruit, neither can a corrupt tree bring forth good fruit. Every tree that bringeth not forth good fruit is hewn down, and cast into the fire. Wherefore by their fruits ye shall know them (Matthew 7:15-20 KJV).

Hear the word of the LORD, ye that tremble at his word; Your brethren that hated you, that cast you out for my name's sake, said, Let the LORD be glorified: but he shall appear to your joy, and they shall be ashamed. A voice of noise from the city, a voice from the temple, a voice of the LORD that rendereth recompence to his enemies (Isaiah 66:5-6 KJV). The wicked have drawn out the sword, and have bent their bow, to cast down the poor and needy, and to slay such as be of upright conversation. Their sword shall enter into their own heart, and their bows shall be broken. A little that a righteous man hath is better than the riches of many wicked. For the arms of the wicked shall be broken: but the LORD upholdeth the righteous (Psalm 37:14-17 KJV). But God shall wound the head of his enemies, and the hairy scalp of such an one as goeth on still in his trespasses (Psalm 68:21 KJV). Lo, these are parts of his ways: but how little a portion is heard of him? but the thunder of his power who can understand? (Job 26:14 KJV).

Ancient Paths

Old wisdom is outdated, but I'm speaking forth its wealth.
They say, "Come and eat and drink," but what they offer teaches stealth.

The LORD knows that they are stingy, but they're handing out what's costly.
But what I found was underhanded, and it was this truth that almost lost me.

What does it mean to dash your foot, to dash your foot against a stone?
If the promise is in their strength, well, then the truth of it is gone.

Do you have to buy or sell if you're going to inherit?
Although they have the means for kindness, the lack of profit will deter it.

What kind of kindness is a kindness if the kindness won't risk loss?
It's because of the way they've gained that He deems them worthless doss.

Ancient Paths

We have heard with our ears, O God, our fathers have told us, what work thou didst in their days, in the times of old. How thou didst drive out the heathen with thy hand, and plantedst them; how thou didst afflict the people, and cast them out. For they got not the land in possession by their own sword, neither did their own arm save them: but thy right hand, and thine arm, and the light of thy countenance, because thou hadst a favour unto them (Psalm 44:1-3 KJV). But thou hast cast off, and put us to shame; and goest not forth with our armies. Thou makest us to turn back from the enemy: and they which hate us spoil for themselves. Thou hast given us like sheep appointed for meat; and hast scattered us among the heathen (Psalm 44:9-11 KJV).

Behold, a king shall reign in righteousness, and princes shall rule in judgment. And a man shall be as an hiding place from the wind, and a covert from the tempest; as rivers of water in a dry place, as the shadow of a great rock in a weary land. And the eyes of them that see shall not be dim, and the ears of them that hear shall hearken. The heart also of the rash shall understand knowledge, and the tongue of the stammerers shall be ready to speak plainly. The vile person shall be no more called liberal, nor the churl said to be bountiful. For the vile person will speak villany, and his heart will work iniquity, to practise hypocrisy, and to utter error against the LORD, to make empty the soul of the hungry, and he will cause the drink of the thirsty to fail. The instruments also of the churl are evil: he deviseth wicked devices to destroy the poor with lying words, even when the needy speaketh right. But the liberal deviseth liberal things; and by liberal things shall he stand (Isaiah 32:1-8 KJV). Shall not they teach thee, and tell thee, and utter words out of their heart (Job 8:10 KJV)? The rich man shall lie down, but he shall not be gathered: he openeth his eyes, and he is not (Job 27:19 KJV).

Fruit of the Spirit: **Meekness**

Romans 8:18-21 KJV

For the earnest expectation of the creature waiteth for the manifestation of the sons of God. For the creature was made subject to vanity, not willingly, but by reason of him who hath subjected the same in hope, because the creature itself also shall be delivered from the bondage of corruption into the glorious liberty of the children of God.

An Early Kiss

What does it mean to kiss the Son? Perhaps it means to obey.
If a kiss won't do the work, well, then what else is left to say?

Could I take pride in my own work and therefore give myself the glory?
Would I be worthy of His writing while I'm telling my own story?

I'm inspired by the Spirit; I'm inspired by His hand.
I live to serve the Master, and this is therefore why I stand.

I stand to serve a kingdom. Can you hear what you have heard?
I've lived a certain truth, which has made me kiss the Word.

This is an honest answer to a service that's provided;
A message to the reader and the righteous that are guided.

They are guided by a process and a certain type of kiss.
The kiss is underway, and it goes something like this:

The lips are to the tongue as the tonsils are to throat.
Let Saliva touch your tongue and thus be healed by what one wrote!

Insight: Psalm 22:15 KJV

An Early Kiss

A garden inclosed is my sister, my spouse; a spring shut up, a fountain sealed. Thy plants are an orchard of pomegranates, with pleasant fruits; camphire, with spikenard, Spikenard and saffron; calamus and cinnamon, with all trees of frankincense; myrrh and aloes, with all the chief spices: A fountain of gardens, a well of living waters, and streams from Lebanon (Song of Solomon 4:12-15 KJV). Thy lips, O my spouse, drop as the honeycomb: honey and milk are under thy tongue; and the smell of thy garments is like the smell of Lebanon (Song of Solomon 4:11 KJV). Let him kiss me with the kisses of his mouth: for thy love is better than wine. Because of the savour of thy good ointments thy name is as ointment poured forth, therefore do the virgins love thee (Song of Solomon 1:2-3 KJV).

Look not upon me, because I am black, because the sun hath looked upon me. I am black, but comely, O ye daughters of Jerusalem, as the tents of Kedar, as the curtains of Solomon (Song of Solomon 1:6,5 KJV). Fear not, O land; be glad and rejoice: for the LORD will do great things. Be not afraid, ye beasts of the field: for the pastures of the wilderness do spring, for the tree beareth her fruit, the fig tree and the vine do yield their strength. Be glad then, ye children of Zion, and rejoice in the LORD your God: for he hath given you the former rain moderately, and he will cause to come down for you the rain, the former rain, and the latter rain in the first month (Joel 2:21-23 KJV). Give ear, O ye heavens, and I will speak; and hear, O earth, the words of my mouth. My doctrine shall drop as the rain, my speech shall distil as the dew, as the small rain upon the tender herb, and as the showers upon the grass: Because I will publish the name of the LORD: ascribe ye greatness unto our God. He is the Rock, his work is perfect: for all his ways are judgment: a God of truth and without iniquity, just and right is he. They have corrupted themselves, their spot is not the spot of his children: they are a perverse and crooked generation (Deuteronomy 32:1-5 KJV).

A Meek Meal

What can this righteous soldier say? My feelings were uneasy.
My openness to closure had me felling kind of sleazy.

I thought I lived the life, but found my death was sacrificial.
I thought I knew a way, but what I knew was superficial.

This was service at high risk. It was a service of a kind.
Because my eyes were opened, it left this servant feeling blind.

I was open to instruction; the instructions came with shock!
I saw Him standing at my door but didn't understand the knock.

He said, "go ahead and come with Me. Let Me drive you to a place.
Let Me show you a new sighting that their vision can't replace."

There was protection in His path, and the path was not detected.
If the choice were up to me, I would have lost my soul protected.

Former guardrails were destroyed. He drove right off the cliff.
He said, "I didn't come to harm you, or to fail you, but to sift."

He guided me in judgment, and He taught me in a way,
That left my soul at ease and put this meekness on display.

A Meek Meal

The meek will he guide in judgment: and the meek will he teach his way. All the paths of the LORD are mercy and truth unto such as keep his covenant and his testimonies. For thy names sake, O LORD, pardon mine iniquity; for it is great. What man is he that feareth the LORD; him shall he teach in the way that he shall choose. His soul shall dwell at ease; and his seed shall inherit the earth (Psalm 25:9-13 KJV). The ungodly are not so: but are like the chaff which the wind driveth away. Therefore the ungodly shall not stand in the judgment, nor sinners in the congregation of the righteous (Psalm 1:4-5 KJV). For every one that doeth evil hateth the light, neither cometh to the light, lest his deeds should be reproved. But he that doeth truth cometh to the light, that his deeds may be made manifest, that they are wrought in God (John 3:20-21 KJV).

And after these things I saw four angels standing on the four corners of the earth, holding the four winds of the earth, that the wind should not blow on the earth, nor on the sea, nor on any tree. And I saw another angel ascending from the east, having the seal of the living God: and he cried with a loud voice to the four angels, to whom it was given to hurt the earth and the sea, Saying, Hurt not the earth, neither the sea, nor the trees, till we have sealed the servants of our God in their foreheads. And I heard the number of them which were sealed: and there were sealed an hundred and forty and four thousand of all the tribes of the children of Israel (Revelation 7: 1-4 KJV). Beloved, follow not that which is evil, but that which is good. He that doeth good is of God: but he that doeth evil hath not seen God (3 John 1:11 KJV).

I Can't Believe My Eyes!

What is this that I'm seeing? I can't believe my eyes!
They tried to hide their insurrection without the scrutiny of the wise.

They privily hid their snares, then they called it what was good.
I'm now indicting evil, repealing judgments as I should.

He hid me from their counsel, and now which men shall fear?
The wicked will be fretful, but let the righteous soldier cheer.

The way they turned the other cheek represented what's egregious.
Their cheekiness was lame; He deemed my lameness as prestigious.

Their prosperity is their prison, their poverty is their jail.
Their gossip spread as lies, but by what's true you couldn't tell.

I almost chose to do some work that would've reflected what was lies.
My faith is without question, seeing the truth of what belies.

What had lied within my heart would force a labor unintended.
The way a heart responds to Light reflects well on His descendants.

He protected me from me. It was up to me. I must receive it.
He answered my decision with, to know, you better believe it!

I Can't Believe My Eyes

Surely thou didst set them in slippery places: thou castedst them down into destruction. How are they brought into desolation, as in a moment! they are utterly consumed with terrors. As a dream when one awaketh; so, O LORD, when thou awakest, thou shalt despise their image (Psalm 73:18-20 KJV). For the LORD spake thus to me with a strong hand, and instructed me that I should not walk in the way of this people, saying, Say ye not, A confederacy, to all them to whom this people shall say, A confederacy; neither fear ye their fear, nor be afraid. Sanctify the LORD of hosts himself; and let him be your fear, and let him be your dread. And he shall be for a sanctuary; but for a stone of stumbling and for a rock of offence to both the houses of Israel, for a gin and for a snare to the inhabitants of Jerusalem. And many among them shall stumble, and fall, and be broken, and be snared, and be taken (Isaiah 8:11-15 KJV).

Blessed is he that considereth the poor: the LORD will deliver him in time of trouble. The LORD will preserve him, and keep him alive; and he shall be blessed upon the earth: and thou wilt not deliver him unto the will of his enemies. The LORD will strengthen him upon the bed of languishing: thou wilt make all his bed in his sickness (Psalm 41:1-3 KJV). Come, ye children, hearken unto me: I will teach you the fear of the LORD. What man is he that desireth life, and loveth many days, that he may see good? Keep thy tongue from evil, and thy lips from speaking guile (Psalm 34:11-13 KJV)! Many are the afflictions of the righteous: but the LORD delivereth him out of them all. He keepeth all his bones: not one of them is broken. Evil shall slay the wicked: and they that hate the righteous shall be desolate (Psalm 34:19-21 KJV).

Eye Messages

Your eyes sent the wrong message to your spirit.
They whispered to your spirit a judgment that didn't fear it.

A pupil is a blind spot without the Eye?
It's a darkness of a light that makes decisions on the fly.

Your eyes sent a message that was unclear,
Because you heard what you didn't see and saw what you didn't hear.

Your eyes didn't keep a close look from within,
So whose heart couldn't hear past the beat of its sin?

Wisdom goes without saying and goes about doing.
Who cares about the "I" when it's your eyes that I'm pursuing?

Eye Messages

But our God is in the heavens: he hath done whatsoever he hath pleased. Their idols are silver and gold, the work of men's hands. They have mouths, but they speak not: eyes have they, but they see not: They have ears, but they hear not: noses have they, but they smell not: They have hands, but they handle not: feet have they, but they walk not: neither speak they through their throat. They that make them are like unto them; so is every one that trusteth in them (Psalm 115:3-8 KJV). Let their table become a snare before them: and that which should have been for their welfare, let it become a trap. Let their eyes be darkened, that they see not; and make their loins continually to shake. Pour out thine indignation upon them, and let thy wrathful anger take hold of them. Let their habitation be desolate; and let none dwell in their tents (Psalm 69:22-25 KJV). The humble shall see this, and be glad: and your heart shall live that seek God (Psalm 69:32 KJV).

And there shall come forth a rod out of the stem of Jesse, and a Branch shall grow out of his roots: And the spirit of the LORD shall rest upon him, the spirit of wisdom and understanding, the spirit of counsel and might, the spirit of knowledge and of the fear of the LORD; And shall make him of quick understanding in the fear of the LORD: and he shall not judge after the sight of his eyes, neither reprove after the hearing of his ears: But with righteousness shall he judge the poor, and reprove with equity for the meek of the earth: and he shall smite the earth: with the rod of his mouth, and with the breath of his lips shall he slay the wicked (Isaiah 11:1-4 KJV). Let thine eyes look right on, and let thine eyelids look straight before thee. Ponder the path of thy feet, and let all thy ways be established. Turn not to the right hand nor to the left: remove thy foot from evil (Proverbs 4:25-27 KJV).

Healthcare

If life and death are married, which role do you choose to play?
If you don't care to be amused, well, then what else is left to say?

There is a yoke that is unequal; it's unequal to My plans.
It represents a jealous spirit and puts envy where it stands.

Their rock had run for office, but their water never ran.
If he could heal them from their sickness, they'd vaccinate against His plan.

They cared about a person. Better yet, who is the third?
There are choices you can make, and He is one, if you have heard?

I cared about another's needs, and so, I put my wealth to work.
I was a needy servant, putting forth my hands to work.

They claimed that I was sickly and my doctrine was uptight.
They tried to sit me down, but I was called to stand upright.

Sorcery is to sickness, just as healing is to light.
The darkness of His mystery is as their knowledge is to night.

Healthcare

Truly God is good to Israel, even to such as are of a clean heart. But as for me, my feet were almost gone; my steps had well nigh slipped. For I was envious at the foolish, when I saw the prosperity of the wicked. For there are no bands in their death: but their strength is firm. They are not in trouble as other men; neither are they plagued like other men. Therefore pride compasseth them about as a chain; violence covereth them as a garment. Their eyes stand out with fatness: they have more than heart could wish. They set their mouth against the heavens, and their tongue walketh through the earth. Therefore his people return hither: and waters of a full cup are wrung out to them (Psalm 73:1-7, 9-10 KJV).

Behold, these are the ungodly, who prosper in the world; they increase in riches. Verily I have cleansed my heart in vain, and washed my hands in innocency. For all the day long have I been plagued, and chastened every morning. If I say, I will speak thus; behold, I should offend against the generation of thy children. When I thought to know this, it was too painful for me; Until I went into the sanctuary of God; then understood I their end (Psalm 73:12-17 KJV). Thus my heart was grieved, and I was pricked in my reins. So foolish was I, and ignorant: I was as a beast before thee. Nevertheless I am continually with thee: thou hast holden me by my right hand. Thou shalt guide me with thy counsel, and afterward receive me to glory. Whom have I in heaven but thee? and there is none upon earth that I desire beside thee. My flesh and my heart faileth: but God is the strength of my heart, and my portion for ever (Psalm 73:24-26 KJV).

Good Bones

I have a bone to pick with riches; riches cheated them of wealth.
If you give a dog a bone, it will defy the commonwealth.

The heritage of the heathen will be given to the "good."
Thy bones have heard His pleasant words; therefore, one has understood.

The wise have waited on the LORD, meanwhile guarding their affairs.
There are some who flaunt their features; they're common aspects of the tares.

When He empties out my storehouse, my inner spirit groans.
All the while He feeds me justice, while making fat thy bones.

Even though I had some freedom, I chose to be proficient.
I didn't see the testing coming, but I trust in the Omniscient.

Who's to say when tests will come? You never know the hand He'll deal.
The cards He gives you may look blank, to assure your character is real.

No failing under pressure. Let the stormy torrents come.
He will bless you with His presence and more gifting and then some.

Build a house through wisdom. It becomes strong through good sense.
Overcome what's insecure, and then your fears will be past tense.

Good Bones

Through wisdom is an house builded; and by understanding it is established: (Proverbs 24:3 KJV). If thou faint in the day of adversity, thy strength is small (Proverbs 24:10 KJV). But I say unto you which hear, Love your enemies, do good to them which hate you, Bless them that curse you, and pray for them which despitefully use you. And unto him that smiteth thee on the one cheek offer also the other; and him that taketh away thy cloak forbid not to take thy coat also. Give to every man that asketh of thee; and of him that taketh away thy goods ask them not again. And as ye would that men should do to you, do ye also to them likewise. For if ye love them which love you, what thank have ye? for sinners also love those that love them. And if ye do good to them which do good to you, what thank have ye? for sinners also do even the same. And if ye lend to them of whom ye hope to receive, what thank have ye? for sinners also lend to sinners, to receive as much again (Luke 6:27-34 KJV).

But love ye your enemies, and do good, and lend, hoping for nothing again; and your reward shall be great, and ye shall be the children of the Highest: for he is kind unto the unthankful and to the evil. Be ye therefore merciful, as your Father also is merciful (Luke 6:35-36 KJV). I said of laughter, It is mad: and of mirth, What doeth it? I sought in mine heart to give myself unto wine, yet acquainting mine heart with wisdom; and to lay hold on folly, till I might see what was that good for the sons of men, which they should do under the heaven all the days of their life (Ecclesiastes 2:2-3 KJV). For there is a man whose labour is in wisdom, and in knowledge, and in equity; yet to a man that hath not laboured therein shall he leave it for his portion. This also is vanity and a great evil. For what hath man of all his labour, and of the vexation of his heart, wherein he hath laboured under the sun? For all his days are sorrows, and his travail grief; yea, his heart taketh not rest in the night. This is also vanity (Ecclesiastes 2:21-23 KJV). 25 For who can eat, or who else can hasten hereunto, more than I (Ecclesiastes 2:25 KJV)?

Trust F.U.N.D.
Faithfulness Under Nostalgic Demand

Faithfulness of deceit is of the world that it demanded.
It has a falsehood in its morals that is often reprimanded.

Condemnation for the wicked and conviction for the Saints,
Who trusted in a way that demanded that one faints?

A fund that is of self is a fund without true wealth,
A faithful faithlessness that serves as a disservice to one's health.

A past that hasn't passed reveals the truth of how one trusted.
A poor manager of truth would rather look at it disgusted.

Lust had been the partner that had never met with candor.
"He divideth flames of fire," revealing faulty propaganda.

Psalm 29:7 KJV

Insight: Psalm 118:8 KJV

It's better to trust in God than to trust in human strength.
Faith that is not measured goes the distance without the length.

Perniciousness seems smooth. He always knew that they would feign.
Whoever's righteous He will guide, and in due time that one will reign.

Trust FUND

He that is faithful in that which is least is faithful also in much: and he that is unjust in the least is unjust also in much. If therefore ye have not been faithful in the unrighteous mammon, who will commit to your trust the true riches? And if ye have not been faithful in that which is another man's, who shall give you that which is your own (Luke 16:10-12 KJV)? "No man can serve two masters: for either he will hate the one, and love the other; or else he will hold to the one, and despise the other. Ye cannot serve God and mammon (Matthew 6:24 KJV). I have many things to say and to judge of you: but he that sent me is true; and I speak to the world those things which I have heard of him (John 8:26 KJV)."

Acquaint now thyself with him, and be at peace: thereby good shall come unto thee. Receive, I pray thee, the law from his mouth, and lay up his words in thine heart. If thou return to the Almighty, thou shalt be built up, thou shalt put away iniquity far from thy tabernacles. Then shalt thou lay up gold as dust, and the gold of Ophir as the stones of the brooks. Yea, the Almighty shall be thy defence, and thou shalt have plenty of silver (Job 22:21-25 KJV). Be not thou afraid when one is made rich, when the glory of his house is increased; For when he dieth he shall carry nothing away: his glory shall not descend after him. Though while he lived he blessed his soul: and men will praise thee, when thou doest well to thyself. He shall go to the generation of his fathers; they shall never see light. Man that is in honour, and understandeth not, is like the beasts that perish (Psalm 49:16-20 KJV). Seek ye the LORD while he may be found, call ye upon him while he is near: Let the wicked forsake his way, and the unrighteous man his thoughts: and let him return unto the LORD, and He will have mercy upon him; and to our God, for he will abundantly pardon. For my thoughts are not your thoughts, neither are your ways my ways, saith the LORD (Isaiah 55:6-8 KJV).

Deceptive Wages

Two different hands within one bowl, and so, who is the double-dipper?
Who takes two sips from this one "cup" that I could call a double-sipper?

Jesus always singles out those He delivers from their sins.
They find their lives have well been written when an ending just begins.

There are details in a mystery that betrayers do not know.
The details hide within what's written, but their pride won't let it show.

If the wages of sin are death, what is life when misaligned?
Unparalleled accounts with due amounts that reassigned.

What flowed abundantly revealed the hidden purpose of the heart.
For the fruit that is NOT good, you'll find within their shopping cart.

They may be rich and prosperous now, and are often getting praise,
But time will truly tell their secrets, both now and in the coming days.

Desire of depth can bring healing; it's known to set a certain stage.
Certain actors are rewarded. Who thought of pleasure as a wage?

What are my wages for receiving all this costly revelation?
He replaces minimum wage with unexpected acclamation.

Deceptive Wages

Blessed are ye that hunger now: for ye shall be filled. Blessed are ye that weep now: for ye shall laugh (Luke 6:21 KJV). But woe unto you that are rich! for ye have received your consolation. Woe unto you that are full! for ye shall hunger. Woe unto you that laugh now! for ye shall mourn and weep. Woe unto you, when all men shall speak well of you! for so did their fathers to the false prophets (Luke 6:24-26 KJV). Shall the throne of iniquity have fellowship with thee, which frameth mischief by a law? They gather themselves together against the soul of the righteous, and condemn the innocent blood (Psalm 94:20-21 KJV).

Behold, a whirlwind of the LORD is gone forth in fury, even a grievous whirlwind: it shall fall grievously upon the head of the wicked. The anger of the LORD shall not return, until he have executed, and till he have performed the thoughts of his heart: in the latter days ye shall consider it perfectly (Jeremiah 23:19-20 KJV). I will also stretch out mine hand upon Judah, and upon all the inhabitants of Jerusalem; and I will cut off the remnant of Baal from this place, and the name of the Chemarims with the priests; And them that worship the host of heaven upon the housetops; and them that worship and that swear by the LORD, and that swear by Malcham; And them that are turned back from the LORD; and those that have not sought the LORD, nor enquired for him (Zephaniah 1:4-6 KJV). If the foundations be destroyed, what can the righteous do (Psalm 11:3 KJV)?

Severance

The poor oppressed the poor, and they reigned without a reverence.
I'm dishing out His justice; who are they to collect a severance?

The godly care about the rights, the rights of those considered poor.
Restricted wealth can meet a need or shed its light on all the more.

Some families come united. They call themselves a packaged deal.
Blind eyes can lead to life, if only knowing looks can kill.

They sow into a system, but the system steals their wealth.
They've planned to end work well that won't contribute to one's health.

He denied my hands the work. Who would think to call it severance?
Those who learn to think much higher learned the skill through proper reverence.

What I thought was me being lazy; He called the thought a stunt.
I heard a truth that couldn't fail; He called the riches of the hunt.

Due diligence was needed, and thus the need had then been met.
The art had then been painted, so it looked like what was whet.

Deny some opportunities if you want to get the seal.
The timing of the matter is put within a packaged deal.

Severance

Hell and destruction are before the LORD: how much more then the hearts of the children of men? A scorner loveth not one that reproveth him: neither will he go unto the wise (Proverbs 15:11-12 KJV). He that reproveth a scorner getteth to himself shame: and he that rebuketh a wicked man getteth himself a blot. Reprove not a scorner, lest he hate thee: rebuke a wise man, and he will love thee. Give instruction to a wise man, and he will be yet wiser: teach a just man, and he will increase in learning. The fear of the LORD is the beginning of wisdom: and the knowledge of the holy is understanding. For by me thy days shall be multiplied, and the years of thy life shall be increased. If thou be wise, thou shalt be wise for thyself: but if thou scornest, thou alone shalt bear it (Proverbs 9:7-12 KJV).

The hand of the diligent shall bear rule: but the slothful shall be under tribute. The slothful man roasteth not that which he took in hunting: but the substance of a diligent man is precious (Proverbs 12:24, 27 KJV). Let all those that seek thee rejoice and be glad in thee: and let such as love thy salvation say continually, Let God be magnified (Psalm 70:4 KJV)!" And I looked, and, lo, a Lamb stood on the mount Sion, and with him an hundred forty and four thousand, having his Father's name written in their foreheads. And I heard a voice from heaven, as the voice of many waters, and as the voice of a great thunder: and I heard the voice of harpers harping with their harps: And they sung as it were a new song before the throne, and before the four beasts, and the elders: and no man could learn that song but the hundred and forty and four thousand, which were redeemed from the earth. These are they which were not defiled with women; for they are virgins. These are they which follow the Lamb whithersoever he goeth. These were redeemed from among men, being the firstfruits unto God and to the Lamb (Revelation 14:1-5 KJV).

Do You Follow?

They say they're about the Father's business, but they're snarling in defiance.
These fools who think they're wise will follow suit without reliance.

Where His foolishness is wiser, the fools wouldn't dare take part.
They'd rather sell their birthrights making money from the start.

Their end is of destruction; He trapped them in their clever schemes.
Although my followers prosper, it's not always how it seems.

The sheep who knew My voice were fools enough to follow Me.
My weakness makes them stronger than their foes if you can see.

Some were quick in their successes, because they did not learn to trust.
Some only appeared to be the fool. Now ~~here~~ hear comes judgment! Eat our dust!

Do You Follow?

Plead my cause, O LORD, with them that strive with me: fight against them that fight against me. Take hold of shield and buckler, and stand up for mine help. Draw out also the spear, and stop the way against them that persecute me: say unto my soul, I am thy salvation. Let them be confounded and put to shame that seek after my soul: let them be turned back and brought to confusion that devise my hurt. Let them be as chaff before the wind: and let the angel of the LORD chase them. Let their way be dark and slippery: and let the angel of the LORD persecute them. For without cause have they hid for me their net in a pit, which without cause they have digged for my soul. Let destruction come upon him at unawares; and let his net that he hath hid catch himself: into that very destruction let him fall (Psalm 35:1-8 KJV). False witnesses did rise up; they laid to my charge things that I knew not. They rewarded me evil for good to the spoiling of my soul (Psalm 35:11-12 KJV).

With hypocritical mockers in feasts, they gnashed upon me with their teeth. Lord, how long wilt thou look on? rescue my soul from their destructions, my darling from the lions. I will give thee thanks in the great congregation: I will praise thee among much people. Let not them that are mine enemies wrongfully rejoice over me: neither let them wink with the eye that hate me without a cause. For they speak not peace: but they devise deceitful matters against them that are quiet in the land (Psalm 35:16-20 KJV). This thou hast seen, O LORD: keep not silence: O LORD, be not far from me. Stir up thyself, and awake to my judgment, even unto my cause, my God and my Lord. Judge me, O LORD my God, according to thy righteousness; and let them not rejoice over me. Let them not say in their hearts, Ah, so would we have it: let them not say, We have swallowed him up. Let them be ashamed and brought to confusion together that rejoice at mine hurt: let them be clothed with shame and dishonour that magnify themselves against me. And my tongue shall speak of thy righteousness and of thy praise all the day long (Psalm 35:22-26, 28 KJV).

Innocent Bystanders

I was feeling somewhat guilty. My thoughts could pass for evil.
Were my thoughts from Satan, or of my own lustful upheaval?

Favour is deceitful; fear the LORD and serve the needy.
When grasping is the method, then a trap becomes the treaty.

My purpose was established. My heart was healed to do the work.
I saw what tried to kill. What is a lie that wouldn't lurk?

He adjusted my position and turned my head to look toward life.
One fang I called a tooth, He said more like a sharpened knife.

I was innocent of willful sin. My mind was unaware.
What I thought was true became the lie I call the tare.

Weaknesses were assessed, but by His strength you couldn't tell.
Perhaps one could conclude my pride was swallowed by a whale.

My mistake had been revealed; My response was up to me.
I was up to being corrected. Truth called out what I could be.

Innocent Bystanders

I rejoice at thy word, as one that findeth great spoil. I hate and abhor lying: but thy law do I love. Great peace have they which love thy law: and nothing shall offend them. My soul hath kept thy testimonies; and I love them exceedingly (Psalm 119:162-163, 165, 167 KJV). I have kept thy precepts and thy testimonies: for all my ways are before thee. Let my cry come near before thee, O LORD: give me understanding according to thy word. My lips shall utter praise, when thou hast taught me thy statutes. My tongue shall speak of thy word: for all thy commandments are righteousness (Psalms 119:168-169, 171-72 KJV).

As the cold of snow in the time of harvest, so is a faithful messenger to them that send him: for he refresheth the soul of his masters (Proverbs 25:13 KJV). Ye call me Master and Lord: and ye say well; for so I am. If I then, your Lord and Master, have washed your feet; ye also ought to wash one another's feet (John 13:13-14 KJV). Go not forth hastily to strive, lest thou know not what to do in the end thereof, when thy neighbour hath put thee to shame (Proverbs 25:8 KJV). For I have given you an example, that ye should do as I have done to you. Verily, verily, I say unto you, The servant is not greater than his lord; neither he that is sent greater than he that sent him. If ye know these things, happy are ye if ye do them (John 13:15-17 KJV). I speak not of you all: I know whom I have chosen: but that the scripture may be fulfilled, He that eateth bread with me hath lifted up his heel against me. Now I tell you before it come, that, when it is come to pass, ye may believe that I am he. Verily, verily, I say unto you, He that receiveth whomsoever I send receiveth me; and he that receiveth me receiveth him that sent me (John 13:18-20 KJV)."

I Stand Corrected

I stand corrected.

I've been chosen and was selected,

To stand out because of what Christ perfected.

The gifts that He gives, I refuse to let go neglected.

I can't be afraid, because I'm protected.

He lifted me up when I was feeling dejected.

I couldn't go along with what they suggested.

I felt in my gut what hadn't digested.

It was the cares of the world that they had ingested.

I had to go without those who hadn't invested,

So that I could live and learn to stand corrected.

I Stand Corrected

Praise ye the LORD. I will praise the LORD with my whole heart, in the assembly of the upright, and in the congregation (Psalm 111:1 KJV). He hath given meat unto them that fear him: he will ever be mindful of his covenant. He hath shewed his people the power of his works, that he may give them the heritage of the heathen (Psalm 111:5-6 KJV). He sent redemption unto his people: he hath commanded his covenant for ever: holy and reverend is his name. The fear of the LORD is the beginning of wisdom: a good understanding have all they that do his commandments: his praise endureth for ever (Psalm 111:9-10 KJV)! Behold, God exalteth by his power: who teacheth like him? Who hath enjoined him his way? or who can say, Thou hast wrought iniquity? Remember that thou magnify his work, which men behold. Every man may see it; man may behold it afar off (Job 36:22-25 KJV)!

I would seek unto God, and unto God would I commit my cause: Which doeth great things and unsearchable; marvellous things without number: Who giveth rain upon the earth, and sendeth waters upon the fields: To set up on high those that be low; that those which mourn may be exalted to safety. He disappointeth the devices of the crafty, so that their hands cannot perform their enterprise. He taketh the wise in their own craftiness: and the counsel of the froward is carried headlong. They meet with darkness in the day time, and grope in the noonday as in the night. But he saveth the poor from the sword, from their mouth, and from the hand of the mighty. So the poor hath hope, and iniquity stoppeth her mouth. Behold, happy is the man whom God correcteth: therefore despise not thou the chastening of the Almighty: For he maketh sore, and bindeth up: he woundeth, and his hands make whole. He shall deliver thee in six troubles: yea, in seven there shall no evil touch thee (Job 5:8-19 KJV).

Guilty Bystanders

They were present but were absent from the presence of correction.
They thought they could counsel malevolent aim without detection.

Their pride won't let them hear what an enemy has to offer,
Unjust judgment of true wisdom, and so they are deemed a scoffer.

Humiliation had a way; it had a way of ending pride.
Because I honored law, it wouldn't let the gifting hide.

Divine guidance led the way and exposed me to what shamed.
What do you call an unknown "child" if it were so to be named?

In reference to: James 1:15 KJV

If the sin had been unknown, could you call the seed what's evil?
Yet they knew what they were hiding, but instead they made it legal.

It was pretense that did them in, along with arrogance playing its role.
How could their business be My business with an un-submitted soul?

They had elaborated plans, in which the plans did come to past.
They appeared to serve Me first but will serve My kingdom last.

Guilty Bystanders

A certain man went down from Jerusalem to Jericho, and fell among thieves, which stripped him of his raiment, and wounded him, and departed, leaving him half dead. And by chance there came down a certain priest that way: and when he saw him, he passed by on the other side. And likewise a Levite, when he was at the place, came and looked on him, and passed by on the other side. But a certain Samaritan, as he journeyed, came where he was: and when he saw him, he had compassion on him, And went to him, and bound up his wounds, pouring in oil and wine, and set him on his own beast, and brought him to an inn, and took care of him. And on the morrow when he departed, he took out two pence, and gave them to the host, and said unto him, Take care of him; and whatsoever thou spendest more, when I come again, I will repay thee (Luke 10:30-35 KJV).

Remember this, and shew yourselves men: bring it again to mind, O ye transgressors (Isaiah 46:8 KJV). Hearken unto me, ye stouthearted, that are far from righteousness: I bring near my righteousness; it shall not be far off, and my salvation shall not tarry: and I will place salvation in Zion for Israel my glory (Isaiah 46:12-13 KJV). And I saw another angel fly in the midst of heaven, having the everlasting gospel to preach unto them that dwell on the earth, and to every nation, and kindred, and tongue, and people, Saying with a loud voice, Fear God, and give glory to him; for the hour of his judgment is come: and worship him that made heaven, and earth, and the sea, and the fountains of waters. And there followed another angel, saying, Babylon is fallen, is fallen, that great city, because she made all nations drink of the wine of the wrath of her fornication. And the third angel followed them, saying with a loud voice, If any man worship the beast and his image, and receive his mark in his forehead, or in his hand, The same shall drink of the wine of the wrath of God, which is poured out without mixture into the cup of his indignation; and he shall be tormented with fire and brimstone in the presence of the holy angels, and in the presence of the Lamb (Revelation 14:6-10 KJV).

Supply and Demand

The poor and needy have a way of placing justice on demand.
The wicked rush to join the sinner; they supply the greedy hand.

The prosperity of the wicked is what I call a withered leaf.
Those with food but yet go hungry is what I call a thriving thief.

With everything the world offers, how do you not crave it?
A living sacrifice was offered. It's on dangerous ground that he will save it.

When you're tempted by the devil, you cannot see what death demands.
Your appetite for certain pleasures is offered in your promised land.

What is a sale without a profit, or should I say without incentive?
A supply without demand, but yet is rich with what's inventive.

If the buyer won't demand, they are guided by the Lifter.
They'll supply the world with truth, which defies the common shifter.

If you cannot comprehend, well, let make it plain and simple.
A birthright was forsaken; Sold for bread and stew of lentils.

Twins are in your womb. Flesh and Spirit/Supply and Demand.
Which set has cleared their conscience with what lived for reprimand?

Supply and Demand

More to be desired are they than gold, yea, than much fine gold: sweeter also than honey and the honeycomb. Moreover by them is thy servant warned: and in keeping of them there is great reward. Who can understand his errors? cleanse thou me from secret faults (Psalm 19:10-12 KJV)? 12 Thou sellest thy people for nought, and dost not increase thy wealth by their price (Psalm 44:12 KJV). Give ear, O my people, to my law: incline your ears to the words of my mouth. I will open my mouth in a parable: I will utter dark sayings of old: Which we have heard and known, and our fathers have told us (Psalm 78:1-3 KJV). For he established a testimony in Jacob, and appointed a law in Israel, which he commanded our fathers, that they should make them known to their children: That the generation to come might know them, even the children which should be born; who should arise and declare them to their children (Psalm 78:5-6 KJV).

And Isaac intreated the LORD for his wife, because she was barren: and the LORD was intreated of him, and Rebekah his wife conceived. And the children struggled together within her; and she said, If it be so, why am I thus? And she went to enquire of the LORD. And the LORD said unto her, Two nations are in thy womb, and two manner of people shall be separated from thy bowels; and the one people shall be stronger than the other people; and the elder shall serve the younger (Genesis 25:21-23 KJV). And the boys grew: and Esau was a cunning hunter, a man of the field; and Jacob was a plain man, dwelling in tents (Genesis 25:27 KJV). And Jacob sod pottage: and Esau came from the field, and he was faint: And Esau said to Jacob, Feed me, I pray thee, with that same red pottage; for I am faint: therefore was his name called Edom. And Jacob said, Sell me this day thy birthright. And Esau said, Behold, I am at the point to die: and what profit shall this birthright do to me? And Jacob said, Swear to me this day; and he sware unto him: and he sold his birthright unto Jacob. Then Jacob gave Esau bread and pottage of lentiles; and he did eat and drink, and rose up, and went his way: thus Esau despised his birthright (Genesis 25:29-34 KJV).

Confusing Waters

I could have guessed He said to give it, but I wanted to withhold.
I wasn't entertaining folly. At least, that's what was told.

I was taught one way was wisdom, but this wisdom was not kindness.
It was a weed that needed killing. My obedience healed my blindness.

He speaks of spiritual wisdom, and He speaks of it as grain.
Two concepts had me questioning if they were one in the same.

If the righteous sell their grain, then they'll pass out weeds for free.
The weeds resemble wheat, but what they offer won't agree.

They won't agree to prosper souls; they won't agree to your salvation.
There's injustice in their hands as they perceive from their palpation.

Waiting for confirmation is not the same as hesitation.
A speedy answer from the Lord was to my soul like medication.

He had given me instructions, the instructions known as waters.
Their kindness is of wickedness and so its reputation totters.

Confusing Waters

The soul of the sluggard desireth, and hath nothing: but the soul of the diligent shall be made fat (Proverbs 13:4 KJV). There is that maketh himself rich, yet hath nothing: there is that maketh himself poor, yet hath great riches. The ransom of a man's life are his riches: but the poor heareth not rebuke (Proverbs 13:7-8 KJV). Ye have not yet resisted unto blood, striving against sin. And ye have forgotten the exhortation which speaketh unto you as unto children, My son, despise not thou the chastening of the Lord, nor faint when thou art rebuked of him: For whom the Lord loveth he chasteneth, and scourgeth every son whom he receiveth. If ye endure chastening, God dealeth with you as with sons; for what son is he whom the father chasteneth not? But if ye be without chastisement, whereof all are partakers, then are ye bastards, and not sons. Furthermore we have had fathers of our flesh which corrected us, and we gave them reverence: shall we not much rather be in subjection unto the Father of spirits, and live? For they verily for a few days chastened us after their own pleasure; but he for our profit, that we might be partakers of his holiness. Now no chastening for the present seemeth to be joyous, but grievous: nevertheless afterward it yieldeth the peaceable fruit of righteousness unto them which are exercised thereby. Wherefore lift up the hands which hang down, and the feeble knees (Hebrews 12:4-11 KJV).

And herein do I exercise myself, to have always a conscience void to offence toward God, and toward men (Acts 24:16 KJV). Which sometime were disobedient, when once the longsuffering of God waited in the days of Noah, while the ark was a preparing, wherein few, that is, eight souls were saved by water. The like figure whereunto even baptism doth also now save us (not the putting away of the filth of the flesh, but the answer of a good conscience toward God,) by the resurrection of Jesus Christ: Who is gone into heaven, and is on the right hand of God; angels and authorities and powers being made subject unto him (1 Peter 3:20-22 KJV). The Spirit of the Lord GOD is upon me; because the LORD hath anointed me to preach good tidings unto the meek; he hath sent me to bind up the brokenhearted, to proclaim liberty to the captives, and the opening of the prison to them that are bound (Isaiah 61:1 KJV). The hand of the diligent shall bear rule: but the slothful shall be under tribute (Proverbs 12:24 KJV).

Public Grain

The public needs the grain; the grain needs a certain freedom.
They demand within a plea, and yet the plea won't offer freedom.

Their judgment of the matter reeks of criminal offense.
They only offer worldly wisdom, which is a rich but poor defense.

What do you call a pillar without His wisdom for decisions?
Their tactics are of old, and yet they call them new provisions.

Are they acting on authority? Do they really need permission?
Whose authority act is met with egotistical ambition?

He's outsourcing for a cause. It hasn't mocked Him as of yet.
There are loopholes in their covenant, and I'll call it strangers' debt.

What is the rule of origin in His truth you call a lie?
If He trades your life for death, would you dare to ask Him why?

Are there barriers in trade, or are they trading barriers?
Who refuses to carry their weight, and yet calls themselves the carriers?

When you see who He's accepted, your jealousy will be insane.
His wisdom dishes out the matter, and He calls it public grain.

Public Grain

Remove not the old landmark; and enter not into the fields of the fatherless: For their redeemer is mighty; he shall plead their cause with thee (Proverbs 23:10-11 KJV). Prepare thy work without, and make it fit for thyself in the field; and afterwards build thine house (Proverbs 24:27 KJV). For the grace of God that bringeth salvation hath appeared to all men, Teaching us that, denying ungodliness and worldly lusts, we should live soberly, righteously, and godly, in this present world; Looking for that blessed hope, and the glorious appearing of the great God and our Saviour Jesus Christ; Who gave himself for us, that he might redeem us from all iniquity, and purify unto himself a peculiar people, zealous of good works (Titus 2:11-14 KJV).

Verily, verily, I say unto you, Except a corn of wheat fall into the ground and die, it abideth alone: but if it die, it bringeth forth much fruit (John 12:24 KJV). The Spirit of the Lord GOD is upon me…To proclaim the acceptable year of the LORD, and the day of vengeance of our God; to comfort all that mourn; To appoint unto them that mourn in Zion, to give unto them beauty for ashes, the oil of joy for mourning, the garment of praise for the spirit of heaviness; that they might be called trees of righteousness, the planting of the LORD, that he might be glorified. And they shall build the old wastes, they shall raise up the former desolations, and they shall repair the waste cities, the desolations of many generations. And strangers shall stand and feed your flocks, and the sons of the alien shall be your plowmen and your vinedressers. But ye shall be named the Priests of the LORD: men shall call you the Ministers of our God: ye shall eat the riches of the Gentiles, and in their glory shall ye boast yourselves. For your shame ye shall have double; and for confusion they shall rejoice in their portion: therefore in their land they shall possess the double: everlasting joy shall be unto them (Isaiah 61:1-7 KJV).

Sell the Grain

Go ahead and buy the truth but don't forget to sell the grain.
Those who worship the destroyer work to build for Him in vain.

What should I call this grain? It's now recognized as corn.
You can hold your peace with profit; an old method has been born.

There was a path to safety, and that path was known as narrow.
There's a king you'll likely serve. Should I really call him Pharaoh?

Some have eaten the bead of Heaven. They've dodged a certain yeast.
They have put their hands to work. These are they I call the priest.

What do you call a servant when she forgets she's been enslaved?
She reaps a harvest after selling everything she's ever craved.

Reference: Luke 12:33 KJV

You can sometimes purchase truth when there are no apparent needs.
The bargain "clouts" at moral judgment; it doesn't recognize the need.

No need to be in sorrow; now's the time to show some couth.
What He's selling is a way that helps His servants purchase truth.

There's a way to overcome, but you'll need to make a choice.
What's strange about a fiction helps the servants learn His voice.

Sell the Grain

He that withholdeth corn, the people shall curse him: but blessing shall be upon the head of him that selleth it (Proverbs 11:26 KJV). Woe to the rebellious children, saith the LORD, that take counsel, but not of me; and that cover with a covering, but not of my spirit, that they may add sin to sin: That walk to go down into Egypt, and have not asked at my mouth; to strengthen themselves in the strength of Pharaoh, and to trust in the shadow of Egypt! Therefore shall the strength of Pharaoh be your shame, and the trust in the shadow of Egypt your confusion (Isaiah 30:1-3 KJV). For his princes were at Zoan, and his ambassadors came to Hanes. They were all ashamed of a people that could not profit them, nor be an help nor profit, but a shame, and also a reproach (Isaiah 30:4-5 KJV).

The burden of the beasts of the south: into the land of trouble and anguish, from whence come the young and old lion, the viper and fiery flying serpent, they will carry their riches upon the shoulders of young asses, and their treasures upon the bunches of camels, to a people that shall not profit them (Isaiah 30:6 KJV). Egyptians shall help in vain, and to no purpose: therefore have I cried concerning this, Their strength is to sit still (Isaiah 30:7 KJV). For thus saith the Lord GOD, the Holy One of Israel; In returning and rest shall ye be saved; in quietness and in confidence shall be your strength: and ye would not (Isaiah 30:15 KJV). He that killeth an ox is as if he slew a man; he that sacrificeth a lamb, as if he cut off a dog's neck; he that offereth an oblation, as if he offered swine's blood; he that burneth incense, as if he blessed an idol. Yea, they have chosen their own ways, and their soul delighteth in their abominations (Isaiah 66:3 KJV).

Fruit of the Spirit: **Longsuffering**

And the smoke of their torment ascendeth up for ever and ever: and they have no rest day nor night, who worship the beast and his image, and whosoever receiveth the mark of his name. Here is the patience of the saints: here are they that keep the commandments of God, and the faith of Jesus (Revelation 14:11-12 KJV).

Red Alert

I'm sounding an alarm! This is a red alert!
Black magic is their source. Certain truths have gone berserk!

The Beast has a system, and I know its inner workings.
I work within My plans without the mind that's of its irkings.

I know of their agendas and I know all of their fields.
Though a thousand fall…I will deliver if one yields.

Reference: Psalm 91:6-7 KJV

I could give you information in which I'd liken to a flood.
Their sword has done its flashing and its color is of blood.

Red Alert

And out of the ground made the LORD God to grow every tree that is pleasant to the sight, and good for food; the tree of life also in the midst of the garden, and the tree of knowledge of good and evil (Genesis 2:9 KJV). And he said, Who told thee that thou wast naked? Hast thou eaten of the tree, whereof I commanded thee that thou shouldest not eat (Genesis 3:11 KJV)?" And the serpent said unto the woman, Ye shall not surely die: For God doth know that in the day ye eat thereof, then your eyes shall be opened, and ye shall be as gods, knowing good and evil (Genesis 3:4-5 KJV)." Their eyes stand out with fatness: they have more than heart could wish. They are corrupt, and speak wickedly concerning oppression: they speak loftily. They set their mouth against the heavens, and their tongue walketh through the earth. Therefore his people return hither: and waters of a full cup are wrung out to them. And they say, How doth God know? and is there knowledge in the most High? Behold, these are the ungodly, who prosper in the world; they increase in riches (Psalm 73:7-12 KJV).

Only the trees which thou knowest that they be not trees for meat, thou shalt destroy and cut them down; and thou shalt build bulwarks against the city that maketh war with thee, until it be subdued (Deuteronomy 20:20 KJV). And after these things I heard a great voice of much people in heaven, saying, Alleluia; Salvation, and glory, and honour, and power, unto the Lord our God: For true and righteous are his judgments: for he hath judged the great whore, which did corrupt the earth with her fornication, and hath avenged the blood of his servants at her hand (Revelation 19:1-2 KJV). And a voice came out of the throne, saying, Praise our God, all ye his servants, and ye that fear him, both small and great (Revelation 19:5 KJV). He is wise in heart, and mighty in strength: who hath hardened himself against him, and hath prospered? Which removeth the mountains, and they know not: which overturneth them in his anger (Job 9:4-5 KJV). Thou hast beset me behind and before, and laid thine hand upon me. Such knowledge is too wonderful for me; it is high, I cannot attain unto it (Psalm 139:5-7 KJV)?

The Tree of Life

He said I stroked of pen; now can you understand this strife?
I've met the stroke of death. I'm writing with the Tree of Life.

They think they're playing truth or dare, but they're living life or death.
The truth would be revealed if He should take away their breath.

I stopped the lie in its tracks. The mouth was begging for a beating.
The fool tried to stand for truth but was begging for a seating.

By the entrapment of the soul, he had exasperated quickly.
There was healing in my words, but my truth had made him sickly.

Who wants a certain validation that will keep them where they are?
When He can give them what they crave and thus outgrow the lie by far.

My truth was my "brother's keeper," but he called it keeping tally?
If you ask me where I found it, I would tell you in the valley.

I didn't shy away from truth when truth exposed my selfish flora.
Even after such a fight, my heart received a joyful Aura.

I knew that I was due; that I was due a certain service.
The Tree of Life had blessed my soul. It took away what made me nervous.

The Tree of Life

I wisdom dwell with prudence, and find out the knowledge of witty inventions (Proverbs 8:12 KJV). I am the rose of Sharon, and the lily of the valleys. As the lily among thorns, so is my love among the daughters (Song of Solomon 2:1-2 KJV). The fig tree putteth forth her green figs, and the vines with the tender grape give a good smell. Arise, my love, my fair one, and come away. O my dove, that art in the clefts of the rock, in the secret places of the stairs, let me see thy countenance, let me hear thy voice; for sweet is thy voice, and thy countenance is comely (Song of Solomon 2:13-14 KJV). Say to them that are of a fearful heart, Be strong, fear not: behold, your God will come with vengeance, even God with a recompence; he will come and save you. Then the eyes of the blind shall be opened, and the ears of the deaf shall be unstopped (Isaiah 35:4-5 KJV).

And the ransomed of the LORD shall return, and come to Zion with songs and everlasting joy upon their heads: they shall obtain joy and gladness, and sorrow and sighing shall flee away (Isaiah 35:10 KJV). The wicked, through the pride of his countenance, will not seek after God: God is not in all his thoughts (Psalm 10:4 KJV)." A fool hath no delight in understanding, but that his heart may discover itself (Proverbs 18:2 KJV). Having the understanding darkened, being alienated from the life of God through the ignorance that is in them, because of the blindness of their heart (Ephesians 4:18 KJV), My beloved is mine, and I am his: he feedeth among the lilies (Song of Solomon 2:16 KJV).

The Art of Patience

How would the art of patience look if you were to wear its suit?
Some feet are known to rush to evil and have a strength that's known as brute.

To envy sinners is a fault that often questions a technique.
My mind had lost some hope, because my path was looking bleak.

I rushed with some decisions, and they cost my safety danger.
My fault was pure impatience that left His wisdom looking stranger.

I saw what they produced. It had me crying, "That's not fair!"
Evil fruit had had its moment, yet they didn't understand the snare.

Yes, they have a taste of freedom, but they don't know that I am good.
They do not taste and see and suffer hardship as they should.

Coals of fire for the hungry; touching heads and heaping embers.
You do not look the part but keep the faith and just remember:

Great faith; clear vision, great gain, big eater.
Humble beginnings, yet rich, great patience, great leader.

The Art of Patience

For we are his workmanship, created in Christ Jesus unto good works, which God hath before ordained that we should walk in them (Ephesians 2:10 KJV). Having abolished in his flesh the enmity, even the law of commandments contained in ordinances; for to make in himself of twain one new man, so making peace; And that he might reconcile both unto God in one body by the cross, having slain the enmity thereby: And came and preached peace to you which were afar off, and to them that were nigh. For through him we both have access by one Spirit unto the Father (Ephesians 2:15-18 KJV).

Ethnic hatred has been dissolved by the crucifixion of his precious body on the cross. The legal code that stood condemning every one of us has now been repealed by his command. His triune essence has made peace between us by starting over—forming one new race of humanity, Jews and non-Jews fused together (Ephesians 2:15 KJV)! Blessed be the LORD God of our fathers, which hath put such a thing as this in the king's heart, to beautify the house of the LORD which is in Jerusalem (Ezra 7:27 KJV). I hate vain thoughts: but thy law do I love. Thou art my hiding place and my shield: I hope in thy word. Depart from me, ye evildoers: for I will keep the commandments of my God (Psalm 119:113-115 KJV). But these, as natural brute beasts, made to be taken and destroyed, speak evil of the things that they understand not; and shall utterly perish in their own corruption (2 Peter 2:12 KJV).

Bipartisan

Policies policing what a certain law supposed.
The law that was of faith became the law that was opposed.

There once was separation that was given by a wall.
The wall was broken down, because His name became the call.

They have agitated passions that speak of peace but shout hostility.
There is a way without perfection that spurns the law of its agility.

Who are the rich and the poor? There's still a vast partition.
They speak of equal measures, but their truths come by omission.

Who's given much and what's required? My knowledge is in history.
Division has to be deciphered, because He words it as a mystery.

The sons of men may gain the world, but they blindly lose their soul.
How can they safeguard truth? Is it walls of perjury they patrol?

Jew and Gentile; life and death, male or female, name the war.
For whosoever will, will nonetheless, be given more.

Bipartisan

My flesh trembleth for fear of thee; and I am afraid of thy judgments (Psalm 119:120 KJV). The entrance of thy words giveth light; it giveth understanding unto the simple. I opened my mouth, and panted: for I longed for thy commandments (Psalm 119:130-131 KJV). Deliver me from the oppression of man: so will I keep thy precepts (Psalm 119:134 KJV). Day and night they go about it upon the walls thereof: mischief also and sorrow are in the midst of it. Wickedness is in the midst thereof: deceit and guile depart not from her streets (Psalm 55:10-11 KJV). To whom shall I speak, and give warning, that they may hear? behold, their ear is uncircumcised, and they cannot hearken: behold, the word of the LORD is unto them a reproach; they have no delight in it. Therefore I am full of the fury of the LORD; I am weary with holding in… (Jeremiah 6:10-11 KJV)!

And their houses shall be turned unto others, with their fields and wives together: for I will stretch out my hand upon the inhabitants of the land, saith the LORD. For from the least of them even unto the greatest of them every one is given to covetousness; and from the prophet even unto the priest every one dealeth falsely. They have healed also the hurt of the daughter of my people slightly, saying, Peace, peace; when there is no peace. Were they ashamed when they had committed abomination? nay, they were not at all ashamed, neither could they blush … (Jeremiah 6:12-15 KJV)! Thus saith the LORD, Stand ye in the ways, and see, and ask for the old paths, where is the good way, and walk therein, and ye shall find rest for your souls. But they said, We will not walk therein. Also I set watchmen over you, saying, Hearken to the sound of the trumpet. But they said, We will not hearken. Therefore hear, ye nations, and know, O congregation, what is among them. Hear, O earth: behold, I will bring evil upon this people, even the fruit of their thoughts, because they have not hearkened unto my words, nor to my law, but rejected it. To what purpose cometh there to me incense from Sheba, and the sweet cane from a far country? your burnt offerings are not acceptable, nor your sacrifices sweet unto me (Jeremiah 6:16-20 KJV).

A False Sense of Urgency

It just might take some patience, but what happens if it doesn't?
The art that was of timing became the art of what it wasn't.

Their arguments had me jumping to conclusions of a sickness.
I'm writing with a steady pace if you can understand my quickness.

I heard, "Go forward and be still," at the sameness of a time.
Was I to seek Him or to guess or purchase wisdom on a dime?

Don't be unglued about the waiting! How can I help this message stick?
The Speed of Light had met its match when Patience "shown" Itself as Quick.

The Spirit quickly passed a judgment as I reckoned with Redeemer.
Answerability paints the truth when you draw out a filthy dreamer.

They increase in all their evils, because they love dishonest gain.
They claim to work to stay United, but they mention Me in vain.

The move was slower than was wanted but was quicker than expected.
What move was made denied His wisdom; what was foolish was selected.

Although the matter is intense, it's not urgency I'm stressing.
Division has its purpose, and for this purpose, I'm redressing.

A False Sense of Urgency

Give ear to my prayer, O God; and hide not thyself from my supplication. Attend unto me, and hear me: I mourn in my complaint, and make a noise; Because of the voice of the enemy, because of the oppression of the wicked: for they cast iniquity upon me, and in wrath they hate me. My heart is sore pained within me: and the terrors of death are fallen upon me. Fearfulness and trembling are come upon me, and horror hath overwhelmed me. And I said, Oh that I had wings like a dove! for then would I fly away, and be at rest. Lo, then would I wander far off, and remain in the wilderness. Selah. I would hasten my escape from the windy storm and tempest. Destroy, O Lord, and divide their tongues: for I have seen violence and strife in the city (Psalm 55:1-9 KJV).

I have likened the daughter of Zion to a comely and delicate woman. The shepherds with their flocks shall come unto her; they shall pitch their tents against her round about; they shall feed every one in his place. Prepare ye war against her; arise, and let us go up at noon. Woe unto us! for the day goeth away, for the shadows of the evening are stretched out. Arise, and let us go by night, and let us destroy her palaces. For thus hath the LORD of hosts said, Hew ye down trees, and cast a mount against Jerusalem: this is the city to be visited; she is wholly oppression in the midst of her. As a fountain casteth out her waters, so she casteth out her wickedness: violence and spoil is heard in her; before me continually is grief and wounds. Be thou instructed, O Jerusalem, lest my soul depart from thee; lest I make thee desolate, a land not inhabited. Thus saith the LORD of hosts, They shall throughly glean the remnant of Israel as a vine: turn back thine hand as a grapegatherer into the baskets (Jeremiah 6:2-9 KJV).

Chop Chop

Who would ever think that He would chop this kind of branch?
I knew the cut would hurt in such a way to make one blanch.

The thought had left me yelling, "LORD, "what kind of fruit is this?"
He said the kind that keeps you absent from an ignorance that's bliss.

They produced a fruit as well, but its fruit was their demise.
They were blessed, but all the while, looked like a curse in its disguise.

If I should have a worthy saying and it be to my defense.
My eyes have overseen; I'm overlooking the offense.

If I should speak with gentleness, would my modesty suffice?
He said that I'll need joy, because this was a sacrifice.

What about this goodness had me muttering, "Oh my?"
I knew that I'd speak truth, but they could deem it as a lie.

What about this move or lack thereof is advantageous?
What's moving me along is a command to be courageous.

Although I do not know the outcome, I know I'll see His goodness.
I will see how He rewards and what is known as its profuseness.

Chop Chop

The voice of the LORD divideth the flames of fire (Psalm 29:7 KJV). When the boughs thereof are withered, they shall be broken off: the women come, and set them on fire: for it is a people of no understanding: therefore he that made them will not have mercy on them, and he that formed them will shew them no favour (Isaiah 27:11 KJV). We then, as workers together with him, beseech you also that ye receive not the grace of God in vain (For he saith, I have heard thee in a time accepted, and in the day of salvation have I succoured thee: behold, now is the accepted time; behold, now is the day of salvation.) Giving no offence in any thing, that the ministry be not blamed: But in all things approving ourselves as the ministers of God, in much patience, in afflictions, in necessities, in distresses (2 Corinthians 6:1-4 KJV).

But in all things approving ourselves as the ministers of God, in much patience, in afflictions, in necessities, in distresses, In stripes, in imprisonments, in tumults, in labours, in watchings, in fastings; By pureness, by knowledge, by long suffering, by kindness, by the Holy Ghost, by love unfeigned, By the word of truth, by the power of God, by the armour of righteousness on the right hand and on the left, By honour and dishonour, by evil report and good report: as deceivers, and yet true; As unknown, and yet well known; as dying, and, behold, we live; as chastened, and not killed; As sorrowful, yet alway rejoicing; as poor, yet making many rich; as having nothing, and yet possessing all things (2 Corinthians 6:4-10 KJV). He shall cause them that come of Jacob to take root: Israel shall blossom and bud, and fill the face of the world with fruit (Isaiah 27:6 KJV)! And it shall come to pass in that day, that the LORD shall beat off from the channel of the river unto the stream of Egypt, and ye shall be gathered one by one, O ye children of Israel. And it shall come to pass in that day, that the great trumpet shall be blown… (Isaiah 27:12-13 KJV).

Foreign Policy

They're without proper visitation, yet they're all up in this bed.
It's a type of immigration, if you can hear just what I said.

They're claiming that they follow, yet they seem to be estranged.
I would show them how they're "leading," if only it could be arranged.

A cup of wealth was looking good, while giving rank and so one sips.
Now they're being rewarded for best honorary lips.

They question how the "poor" can hear Me without answering my call.
There's a type of poor that's chosen to make the mighty mountains fall.

I have a policy that's foreign to the wicked soul that prospers.
The righteous work for wisdom; they keep taking what it offers.

I've heard them speak of You, and I'll admit it's kind of scary.
If I hinted at a difference, I would roar out, "SMOOTH AND HAIRY!"

I'm sometimes hairy to the wicked; and to the righteous soul, I'm smooth.
When the righteous need a hand, then it's with hairiness that I soothe.

Rebuke the wise, and they are wiser; they love the way this song is sung.
They question your convention with the wise answer of the tongue.

Foreign Policy

Thus saith the LORD my God; Feed the flock of the slaughter; Whose possessors slay them, and hold themselves not guilty: and they that sell them say, Blessed be the LORD; for I am rich: and their own shepherds pity them not. For I will no more pity the inhabitants of the land, saith the LORD: but, lo, I will deliver the men every one into his neighbour's hand, and into the hand of his king: and they shall smite the land, and out of their hand I will not deliver them. And I will feed the flock of slaughter, even you, O poor of the flock. And I took unto me two staves; the one I called Beauty, and the other I called Bands; and I fed the flock. Three shepherds also I cut off in one month; and my soul lothed them, and their soul also abhorred me. Then said I, I will not feed you: that that dieth, let it die; and that that is to be cut off, let it be cut off; and let the rest eat every one the flesh of another (Zechariah 11:4-9 KJV)!"

And I took my staff, even Beauty, and cut it asunder, that I might break my covenant which I had made with all the people. And it was broken in that day: and so the poor of the flock that waited upon me knew that it was the word of the LORD. And I said unto them, If ye think good, give me my price; and if not, forbear. So they weighed for my price thirty pieces of silver (Zechariah 11:10-12 KJV). Then I cut asunder mine other staff, even Bands, that I might break the brotherhood between Judah and Israel. And the LORD said unto me, Take unto thee yet the instruments of a foolish shepherd. For, lo, I will raise up a shepherd in the land, which shall not visit those that be cut off, neither shall seek the young one, nor heal that that is broken, nor feed that that standeth still: but he shall eat the flesh of the fat, and tear their claws in pieces. Woe to the idol shepherd that leaveth the flock! the sword shall be upon his arm, and upon his right eye: his arm shall be clean dried up, and his right eye shall be utterly darkened (Zechariah 11:14-17 KJV)."

Oh My Goodness!

He confirmed it once again! I can embrace all that I am.
Who knew that the instructions were in a way such as a dam?

I had asked the LORD a question, and the answer was His joy.
The calling manifested in a way that I'd enjoy.

If his goodness was this good, what made me not embrace it?
If you would put it into words; *reflect my heart*, would I erase it?

Psalm 18:27 NLT

He rescued me to see. He humiliates the proud.
They claimed to follow God, but they were following the crowd.

I heard one speak of peace? What was the source that had impelled?
The truth one thought they had, had been a falsehood that had veiled.

He also cut me off from me. You could say I was devoid.
Although He did remove my "spot," I was a servant still employed.

All my goodness came from Him! I'm created for good works!
The narrow well has made its offer. Who's captivated by what lurks?

Words that almost sound accusing are offered by who is begrudging.
Who has wounds without a cause and red eyes if I'm not judging?

Oh my Goodness

Give unto the LORD, O ye mighty, give unto the LORD glory and strength. Give unto the LORD the glory due unto his name; worship the LORD in the beauty of holiness (Psalm 29:1-2 KJV). Every branch in me that beareth not fruit he taketh away: and every branch that beareth fruit, he purgeth it, that it may bring forth more fruit. Now ye are clean through the word which I have spoken unto you. Abide in me, and I in you. As the branch cannot bear fruit of itself, except it abide in the vine; no more can ye, except ye abide in me (John 15:2-4 KJV). I am the vine, ye are the branches: He that abideth in me, and I in him, the same bringeth forth much fruit: for without me ye can do nothing. If a man abide not in me, he is cast forth as a branch, and is withered; and men gather them, and cast them into the fire, and they are burned. If ye abide in me, and my words abide in you, ye shall ask what ye will, and it shall be done unto you. Herein is my Father glorified, that ye bear much fruit; so shall ye be my disciples (John 15:5-8 KJV).

When thou saidst, Seek ye my face; my heart said unto thee, Thy face, LORD, will I seek. Hide not thy face far from me; put not thy servant away in anger: thou hast been my help; leave me not, neither forsake me, O God of my salvation. When my father and my mother forsake me, then the LORD will take me up. Teach me thy way, O LORD, and lead me in a plain path, because of mine enemies. Deliver me not over unto the will of mine enemies: for false witnesses are risen up against me, and such as breathe out cruelty. I had fainted, unless I had believed to see the goodness of the LORD in the land of the living. Wait on the LORD: be of good courage, and he shall strengthen thine heart: wait, I say, on the LORD (Psalm 27: 8-14 KJV). The voice of the LORD is upon the waters: The God of glory thundereth: the LORD is upon many waters (Psalm 29:3 KJV).

The High Road or Narrow Path

The high road is not the same. It is not the narrow path.
The difference is the cost. I should know, I did the math.

Which body part is missing? Is it the finger or the toe?
The narrow path can do the healing. Now you're in the know.

They come in their own name; they're mystified by what's restricted.
Because they're high and mighty, it's by their hand that one's afflicted.

There's a reason that the high road turns its nose up at the narrow.
It cannot get the glory if His eye is on the sparrow.

He's mocking at their truth. Should I call it Glory Road?
I'm driving down a lane, and my speed is up to code.

They may portray a truth with a play on twisted words.
When their falsehood sells for nothing, He'll say, "Tell it to the birds."

They may try to hold me back, but I'll say, "Catch me if you can."
The chase is on a course that He attributes to a plan.

Getting even had its way after all was said and done.
They tried to take my high position, and the odds were slim to none.

The High Road or Narrow Path

And thou shalt say to the rebellious, even to the house of Israel, Thus saith the Lord GOD; O ye house of Israel, let it suffice you of all your abominations, In that ye have brought into my sanctuary strangers, uncircumcised in heart, and uncircumcised in flesh, to be in my sanctuary, to pollute it, even my house, when ye offer my bread, the fat and the blood, and they have broken my covenant because of all your abominations. And ye have not kept the charge of mine holy things: but ye have set keepers of my charge in my sanctuary for yourselves. Thus saith the Lord GOD; No stranger, uncircumcised in heart, nor uncircumcised in flesh, shall enter into my sanctuary, of any stranger that is among the children of Israel (Ezekiel 44:6-9 KJV). And they shall teach my people the difference between the holy and profane, and cause them to discern between the unclean and the clean (Ezekiel 44:23 KJV). Enter ye in at the strait gate: for wide is the gate, and broad is the way, that leadeth to destruction, and many there be which go in thereat: (Matthew 7:13 KJV).

For thus saith the high and lofty One that inhabiteth eternity, whose name is Holy; I dwell in the high and holy place, with him also that is of a contrite and humble spirit, to revive the spirit of the humble, and to revive the heart of the contrite ones. For I will not contend for ever, neither will I be always wroth: for the spirit should fail before me, and the souls which I have made. For the iniquity of his covetousness was I wroth, and smote him: I hid me, and was wroth, and he went on frowardly in the way of his heart. I have seen his ways, and will heal him: I will lead him also, and restore comforts unto him and to his mourners. I create the fruit of the lips; Peace, peace to him that is far off, and to him that is near, saith the LORD; and I will heal him. But the wicked are like the troubled sea, when it cannot rest, whose waters cast up mire and dirt. There is no peace, saith my God, to the wicked (Isaiah 57:15-21 KJV)! Let their table become a snare before them: and that which should have been for their welfare, let it become a trap (Psalms 69:22 KJV).

Behind the Seens

Behind the seens is a spirit,
And a voice that spoke, but you didn't hear it.

It was a voice that spoke life, while you spoke death.
You refused to open up and receive His breath.

Behind the seens is a heart that's crushed,
And pride that brought forth what impatient rushed.

Because what you couldn't see was behind the scenes,
And how the seens played on what seems true.
If you can't see behind the seens, you don't really know you.

Behind the scenes lies lies.
Behind the seens try tries to cover up what's behind the seens.

Behind the Seens

Shall even he that hateth right govern? and wilt thou condemn him that is most just? Is it fit to say to a king, Thou art wicked? and to princes, Ye are ungodly? How much less to him that accepteth not the persons of princes, nor regardeth the rich more than the poor? for they all are the work of his hands. In a moment shall they die, and the people shall be troubled at midnight, and pass away: and the mighty shall be taken away without hand. For his eyes are upon the ways of man, and he seeth all his goings (Job 34:17-21 KJV). Pride goeth before destruction, and an haughty spirit before a fall (Proverbs 16:18 KJV). The lofty looks of man shall be humbled, and the haughtiness of men shall be bowed down, and the LORD alone shall be exalted in that day. For the day of the LORD of hosts shall be upon every one that is proud and lofty, and upon every one that is lifted up; and he shall be brought low (Isaiah 2:11-12 KJV).

There is no darkness, nor shadow of death, where the workers of iniquity may hide themselves. For he will not lay upon man more than right; that he should enter into judgment with God. He shall break in pieces mighty men without number, and set others in their stead. Therefore he knoweth their works, and he overturneth them in the night, so that they are destroyed. He striketh them as wicked men in the open sight of others; Because they turned back from him, and would not consider any of his ways: So that they cause the cry of the poor to come unto him, and he heareth the cry of the afflicted. When he giveth quietness, who then can make trouble? and when he hideth his face, who then can behold him? whether it be done against a nation, or against a man only: That the hypocrite reign not, lest the people be ensnared (Job 34:22-30 KJV)."

Apostrophe

What system is weakened by an apostrophe?
Who would think a small mark could cause an atrocity?

If every language has a meaning, its punctuation has a power.
What kind of mark is known to separate the hour?

If the "match" was made in Heaven, what is a match without a list?
Heaven made its fire, and now Hell has met its fist.

The poor had announced such a coming apostacy.
Before moving forward, let's get back to the apostrophe.

Apostrophe

There are, it may be, so many kinds of voices in the world, and none of them is without signification (1 Corinthians 14:10 KJV). Your fathers, where are they? and the prophets, do they live for ever? But my words and my statutes, which I commanded my servants the prophets, did they not take hold of your fathers? and they returned and said, Like as the LORD of hosts thought to do unto us, according to our ways, and according to our doings, so hath he dealt with us (Zechariah 1:5-6 KJV)." When I shall receive the congregation I will judge uprightly. The earth and all the inhabitants thereof are dissolved: I bear up the pillars of it. Selah (Psalm 75:2-3 KJV).

I said unto the fools, Deal not foolishly: and to the wicked, Lift not up the horn: Lift not up your horn on high: speak not with a stiff neck. For promotion cometh neither from the east, nor from the west, nor from the south. But God is the judge: he putteth down one, and setteth up another. For in the hand of the LORD there is a cup, and the wine is red; it is full of mixture; and he poureth out of the same: but the dregs thereof, all the wicked of the earth shall wring them out, and drink them. But I will declare for ever; I will sing praises to the God of Jacob. All the horns of the wicked also will I cut off; but the horns of the righteous shall be exalted (Psalm 75:4-10 KJV)!

Fruit of the Spirit: **Joy**

And now shall mine head be lifted up above mine enemies round about me: therefore will I offer in his tabernacle sacrifices of joy; I will sing, yea, I will sing praises unto the LORD (Psalm 27:6 KJV).

Do the Math

How do you explain opposing truths that are the same?
One perspective points to Heaven, while the other points to blame.

The pattern on the cup is still the same when upside down.
But when it's right side up, it's known to hold a substance down.

What is feminism? Is it of substance on its own?
What position does one hold when it's My name that "they" disown?

If the first shall be last, what is really to be earned?
What have I subtracted when the table has been turned?

If the cup was upside down and was without being on the table,
I would call the cup a footstool, if I should give the cup a label.

If we understood the "throne" and compared it to His prior,
We would rightly divide the word and would show His ways are higher.

He turns the world right upside down, as those who're on His holy path.
You would receive this calculation, if you would learn to do the math.

Do the Math

Their line is gone out through all the earth, and their words to the end of the world. In them hath he set a tabernacle for the sun, Which is as a bridegroom coming out of his chamber, and rejoiceth as a strong man to run a race. His going forth is from the end of the heaven, and his circuit unto the ends of it: and there is nothing hid from the heat thereof (Psalm 19:4-6 KJV). Hearken, O daughter, and consider, and incline thine ear; forget also thine own people, and thy father's house; So shall the king greatly desire thy beauty: for he is thy Lord; and worship thou him (Psalm 45:10-11 KJV). For thy Maker is thine husband; the LORD of hosts is his name; and thy Redeemer the Holy One of Israel; The God of the whole earth shall he be called. For the LORD hath called thee as a woman forsaken and grieved in spirit, and a wife of youth, when thou wast refused, saith thy God (Isaiah 54:5-6 KJV).

Lift up your heads, O ye gates; and be ye lift up, ye everlasting doors; and the King of glory shall come in. Who is this King of glory? The LORD strong and mighty, the LORD mighty in battle. Lift up your heads, O ye gates; even lift them up, ye everlasting doors; and the King of glory shall come in. Who is this King of glory? The LORD of hosts, he is the King of glory. Selah (Psalm 24:7-10 KJV). Draw out also the spear, and stop the way against them that persecute me: say unto my soul, I am thy salvation (Psalm 35:3 KJV)!" But judgment shall return unto righteousness: and all the upright in heart shall follow it (Psalm 94:15 KJV). I will run the way of thy commandments, when thou shalt enlarge my heart (Psalm 119:32 KJV). But these, as natural brute beasts, made to be taken and destroyed, speak evil of the things that they understand not; and shall utterly perish in their own corruption; And shall receive the reward of unrighteousness, as they that count it pleasure to riot in the day time. Spots they are and blemishes, sporting themselves with their own deceivings while they feast with you (2 Peter 2:12-13 KJV).

Square Root?

God knows how to look at a box and call it a square.
If He insulted your intelligence, would you hear enough to care?

Let's divide the word and take knowledge out of the equation.
Let His truth times the table, and let His wisdom do the suasion.

If being squared is the root, and knowledge puffeth up,
Subtract your held position; it keeps your head from blowing up.

As I followed His instructions, He had my troubles squared away.
And now His judgments are coming, if I should so care to say.

There's a riddle in this number. Is it called denying the power?
If my numbers are correct, that means the grace of wisdom towers.

How do powers play a role if they're imaginary numbers?
They've multiplied by falsehood as a unit, so one slumbers.

What's adverse about an increase when they think they're in the ~~hole~~ whole?
What's complex about the issue is a matter of the soul.

If you can taste this shepherd's pie, you have come upon a zeal.
You leave showing work behind in an *effort* to get real.

Square Root

For who hath stood in the counsel of the LORD, and hath perceived and heard his word? who hath marked his word, and heard it (Jeremiah 23:18 KJV)? Woe be unto the pastors that destroy and scatter the sheep of my pasture! saith the LORD (Jeremiah 23:1 KJV). O Lord God, to whom vengeance belongeth; O God, to whom vengeance belongeth, shew thyself. Lift up thyself, thou judge of the earth: render a reward to the proud. LORD, how long shall the wicked, how long shall the wicked triumph? How long shall they utter and speak hard things? and all the workers of iniquity boast themselves? They break in pieces thy people, O LORD, and afflict thine heritage. They slay the widow and the stranger, and murder the fatherless. Yet they say, The LORD shall not see, neither shall the God of Jacob regard it. Understand, ye brutish among the people: and ye fools, when will ye be wise (Psalm 94:1-8 KJV)?

Can any hide himself in secret places that I shall not see him? saith the LORD. Do not I fill heaven and earth? saith the LORD (Jeremiah 23:24 KJV). He that planted the ear, shall he not hear? he that formed the eye, shall he not see? He that chastiseth the heathen, shall not he correct? he that teacheth man knowledge, shall not he know? The LORD knoweth the thoughts of man, that they are vanity (Psalm 94:9-11 KJV). Therefore, behold, I am against the prophets, saith the LORD, that steal my words every one from his neighbour. Behold, I am against the prophets, saith the LORD, that use their tongues, and say, He saith. Behold, I am against them that prophesy false dreams, saith the LORD, and do tell them, and cause my people to err by their lies, and by their lightness; yet I sent them not, nor commanded them: therefore they shall not profit this people at all, saith the LORD (Jeremiah 23:30-32 KJV)!

The Oil of Joy

What is that I'm feeling? Because it's not the oil of joy.
I know that work is coming, but I would rather not employ.

He said: "that's why I slowed you down. you were not fully rested."
Your heart could not receive the fullness in all the ways I had it tested.

Although I passed with flying colors, my dreams were colorblind.
He covered me with oil, but it was joy He couldn't find.

I didn't have joy. I didn't have strength. My knees were known as feeble.
A lack of understanding can make the Spirit pass for evil.

I didn't know His joy. In my weakness, strength complained.
My spirit had said, "Yes." What made my efforts seem deranged?

Discipline was needed. I had to learn to service rightly.
It was not wrongness He corrected; the heaviness of darkness served me lightly.

The sun has shined upon my darkness. You can say that Joy has risen.
His finger touched my heart. You can say I'm out of prison.

His word is on my mind. Should I be labeled truth fanatic?
I'm now solving "word" problems in light of His mathematics.

The Oil of Joy

I cried unto the LORD with my voice; with my voice unto the LORD did I make my supplication. I poured out my complaint before him; I shewed before him my trouble. When my spirit was overwhelmed within me, then thou knewest my path. In the way wherein I walked have they privily laid a snare for me (Psalm 142:1-3 KJV). Attend unto my cry; for I am brought very low: deliver me from my persecutors; for they are stronger than I. Bring my soul out of prison, that I may praise thy name: the righteous shall compass me about; for thou shalt deal bountifully with me (Psalm 142:6-7 KJV). Praise waiteth for thee, O God, in Sion: and unto thee shall the vow be performed. O thou that hearest prayer, unto thee shall all flesh come. Iniquities prevail against me: as for our transgressions, thou shalt purge them away. Blessed is the man whom thou choosest, and causest to approach unto thee, that he may dwell in thy courts: we shall be satisfied with the goodness of thy house, even of thy holy temple. By terrible things in righteousness wilt thou answer us, O God of our salvation; who art the confidence of all the ends of the earth, and of them that are afar off upon the sea (Psalm 65:1-5 KJV).

For whom the Lord loveth he chasteneth, and scourgeth every son whom he receiveth. If ye endure chastening, God dealeth with you as with sons; for what son is he whom the father chasteneth not? But if ye be without chastisement, whereof all are partakers, then are ye bastards, and not sons. Furthermore we have had fathers of our flesh which corrected us, and we gave them reverence: shall we not much rather be in subjection unto the Father of spirits, and live? For they verily for a few days chastened us after their own pleasure; but he for our profit, that we might be partakers of his holiness. Now no chastening for the present seemeth to be joyous, but grievous: nevertheless afterward it yieldeth the peaceable fruit of righteousness unto them which are exercised thereby. Wherefore lift up the hands which hang down, and the feeble knees; And make straight paths for your feet, lest that which is lame be turned out of the way; but let it rather be healed (Hebrews 12:6-13 KJV).

"Word" Problems

In Light of Mathematics, while breaking "Perfect" Rules

Linear Homogenous differential separable first order equation

Fused Framework: $(x + y)\dfrac{dy}{dx} = x - y$ **&** $\dfrac{dy}{dx} + P(X) \cdot Y = Q(X)$

*Fusing the ideas from the above equations allowed me to create the following:

$F(X) = $ Gn. 1:26-31^4 RT^4-Ro. 7:5^4

Mt. 5:17 AMP

$F(X) = $ Gn. 1:26-31^6 RT^6-Ro. 7:5^6

Mt. 5:17 AMP

(d)Y^4+(P)4XY^4-X(Q)^4=∫ e$^{mt.25:31-26}$

(d)Y^6+(P)4XY^6-X(Q)^6=∫ e$^{jude.1:7\ KJV}$

P= Presence

Q= Quality

RT = Revelation thru Translation

d = Accurately dividing the word of God: *2 Timothy 2:14-26*

Y= Your heart

X= law

$e^{f(x)}$= Represents the Eternal God and Eternal life: *Matthew 25:31-46*

444= Covenant of Life: lim f(x)=444

444= Psalm 119:96

666= Covenant of Death

$$\lim_{n \to 1pt.1:5}$$

Function Tables

Input (X)	Input (Y)
444	**444**
Divine Law	Love
Knowledge	Joy
Wisdom	Peace
Understanding	Longsuffering
Counsel	Meekness
Might	Goodness
Fear of God	Faith
Spirit of God	Temperance
Boldness	Gentleness

Input (X)	Input (Y)
666	**666**
Law	Lust/selfish love
Knowledge	Happiness
Wisdom	Peace
Understanding	Longsuffering
Counsel	Meekness
Might	Goodness
Fear or Man	Unfaithfulness
Flesh	Pious Self-denial

Math Rules	Terms
Reciprocal Rule	Luke 6:35 AMP
Power rule	Zechariah 4:6
Constant Rule	Dt. 28:33, 66 & Ps. 119:98
Chain Rule	Ps. 2:2-4; Ecc. 7:26
Trust Rule	Ps. 131:1-3Peace
Product Rule	2 Peter 1:5-11 VOICE
Faith Rule	Matthew 17:20

"Word" Problems

The people that walked in darkness have seen a great light: they that dwell in the land of the shadow of death, upon them hath the light shined. Thou hast multiplied the nation, and not increased the joy: they joy before thee according to the joy in harvest, and as men rejoice when they divide the spoil. For thou hast broken the yoke of his burden, and the staff of his shoulder, the rod of his oppressor, as in the day of Midian. For every battle of the warrior is with confused noise, and garments rolled in blood; but this shall be with burning and fuel of fire. For unto us a child is born, unto us a son is given: and the government shall be upon his shoulder: and his name shall be called Wonderful, Counsellor, The mighty God, The everlasting Father, The Prince of Peace (Isaiah 9:2-6 KJV).

Of the increase of his government and peace there shall be no end, upon the throne of David, and upon his kingdom, to order it, and to establish it with judgment and with justice from henceforth even for ever. The zeal of the LORD of hosts will perform this (Isaiah 9:7 KJV). If any man have an ear, let him hear. He that leadeth into captivity shall go into captivity: he that killeth with the sword must be killed with the sword. Here is the patience and the faith of the saints (Revelation 13:9-10 KJV). And he causeth all, both small and great, rich and poor, free and bond, to receive a mark in their right hand, or in their foreheads: And that no man might buy or sell, save he that had the mark, or the name of the beast, or the number of his name. Here is wisdom. Let him that hath understanding count the number of the beast: for it is the number of a man; and his number is Six hundred threescore and six (Revelation 13:16-18 KJV). Brethren, if a man be overtaken in a fault, ye which are spiritual, restore such an one in the spirit of meekness; considering thyself, lest thou also be tempted (Galatians 6:1 KJV).

Defying the Odds

Homonyms

Homographs

Homophones

Heterographs

Heteronym

444 English language

The Unspeakable

I may not write in Hebrew, but I write His words with clarity.
What does a language mean to Me if it cannot act as charity?

They claim they have My language, but their mouths are full of gravel.
A certain love receives a tongue, just as the seed is known to travel.

He is a Tower of salvation, but their tower is of Babel.
It would read as, *Such and Such*, if I should give the mess a label.

If even prophecy will end, how should my glory be expressed?
I write from a low degree on which His glory has impressed.

What does it mean to blur, to blur a period with a decimal?
If this number's up to par, it makes this "letter" infinitesimal.

If even perfection has its limit, well, then I've put it into rhymes.
A certain law is up to me, and I've put it in these lines.

There are imaginary numbers; what are imaginary letters?
They are pits that have been dug, but not to free them, so He fetters.

I am a complex number, and I'm living as a hero.
You could say that I'm the one who's been divided by a zero.

The Unspeakable

For the lips of a strange woman drop as an honeycomb, and her mouth is smoother than oil: But her end is bitter as wormwood, sharp as a two-edged sword. Her feet go down to death; her steps take hold on hell. Lest thou shouldest ponder the path of life, her ways are moveable, that thou canst not know them (Proverbs 5:3-6 KJV). But your iniquities have separated between you and your God, and your sins have hid his face from you, that he will not hear. For your hands are defiled with blood, and your fingers with iniquity; your lips have spoken lies, your tongue hath muttered perverseness (Isaiah 59:2-3 KJV). Their poison is like the poison of a serpent: they are like the deaf adder that stoppeth her ear; Which will not hearken to the voice of charmers, charming never so wisely. Break their teeth, O God, in their mouth: break out the great teeth of the young lions, O LORD (Psalm 58:4-6 KJV)!

Let them melt away as waters which run continually: when he bendeth his bow to shoot his arrows, let them be as cut in pieces. As a snail which melteth, let every one of them pass away: like the untimely birth of a woman, that they may not see the sun. Before your pots can feel the thorns, he shall take them away as with a whirlwind, both living, and in his wrath (Psalm 58:7-9 KJV). Woe to them that go down to Egypt for help; and stay on horses, and trust in chariots, because they are many; and in horsemen, because they are very strong; but they look not unto the Holy One of Israel, neither seek the LORD! Yet he also is wise, and will bring evil, and will not call back his words: but will arise against the house of the evildoers, and against the help of them that work iniquity. Now the Egyptians are men, and not God; and their horses flesh, and not spirit. When the LORD shall stretch out his hand, both he that helpeth shall fall, and he that is holpen shall fall down, and they all shall fail together (Isaiah 31:1-3 KJV). Turn ye unto him from whom the children of Israel have deeply revolted. For in that day every man shall cast away his idols of silver, and his idols of gold, which your own hands have made unto you for a sin (Isaiah 31:6-7 KJV).

From Proper to Prosper English

There's something about proper that is incorrect,
Because it can't see past its own intellect.

Proper doesn't understand Prosper,
Because it tries to stop him or her from using the Word correctly.

Proper doesn't understand Prosper's meaning.
It was on its own understanding that it was leaning.

You see,

Prosper told me that it was leaning on the Word,
Of what proper told me that it hadn't heard.

Because it didn't understand what the word was saying.

From Proper to Prosper English

For it is written, I will destroy the wisdom of the wise, and will bring to nothing the understanding of the prudent (1 Corinthians1:19 KJV). Moreover he said unto me, Son of man, eat that thou findest; eat this roll, and go speak unto the house of Israel. So I opened my mouth, and he caused me to eat that roll. And he said unto me, Son of man, cause thy belly to eat, and fill thy bowels with this roll that I give thee. Then did I eat it; and it was in my mouth as honey for sweetness. And he said unto me, Son of man, go, get thee unto the house of Israel, and speak with my words unto them. For thou art not sent to a people of a strange speech and of an hard language, but to the house of Israel; Not to many people of a strange speech and of an hard language, whose words thou canst not understand. Surely, had I sent thee to them, they would have hearkened unto thee (Ezekiel 3:1-6 KJV).

But the house of Israel will not hearken unto thee; for they will not hearken unto me: for all the house of Israel are impudent and hardhearted. Behold, I have made thy face strong against their faces, and thy forehead strong against their foreheads. As an adamant harder than flint have I made thy forehead: fear them not, neither be dismayed at their looks, though they be a rebellious house (Ezekiel 3:7-9 KJV)." For the preaching of the cross is to them that perish foolishness; but unto us which are saved it is the power of God (1 Corinthians 1:18 KJV). Where is the wise? where is the scribe? where is the disputer of this world? hath not God made foolish the wisdom of this world? For after that in the wisdom of God the world by wisdom knew not God, it pleased God by the foolishness of preaching to save them that believe (1 Corinthian 1:20-21 KJV). Because the foolishness of God is wiser than men; and the weakness of God is stronger than men (1 Corinthians 1:25 KJV).

Ride the Donkey!

If He said to ride the donkey, does that mean just play the fool?
Know that you're riding on the "why," and it's to help you learn to rule.

But know that you can only ride it if you learn to kiss it first.
Can they make it through the desert, Lord, or will they die of thirst?

Isaiah 30:20 KJV
Adversity was my food, and affliction was my drink.
I was learning of His truth, not in a way that one would think.

Did the waters turn against me in such a way that I would sink?
The time for change had come, quicker than the eyes could blink.

If I'm coming in a manner not in a way that one would think,
Who will choose to die of thirst and refuse my wine to drink?

Those who've tasted His mixed drink have tasted something that's organic.
But, peace and wickedness have kissed; should this be labeled Sycophantic?

If the world is smart enough to learn to think outside the box,
That means the "Word" is wise enough to know the context and its fox.

Outside of context you might find a hidden truth or hidden treasure.
The thought is up to you, if it's your choice then what's your pleasure?

Ride the Donkey!

Moreover by them is thy servant warned: and in keeping of them there is great reward. Who can understand his errors? cleanse thou me from secret faults. Keep back thy servant also from presumptuous sins; let them not have dominion over me: then shall I be upright, and I shall be innocent from the great transgression. Let the words of my mouth, and the meditation of my heart, be acceptable in thy sight, O LORD, my strength, and my redeemer (Psalm 19:11-14 KJV). Let the brother of low degree rejoice in that he is exalted. Blessed is the man that endureth temptation: for when he is tried, he shall receive the crown of life, which the Lord hath promised to them that love him (James 1:9, 12 KJV). Praise ye the LORD. Blessed is the man that feareth the LORD, that delighteth greatly in his commandments. Wealth and riches shall be in his house: and his righteousness endureth for ever (Psalm 112:1, 3 KJV).

The king's heart is in the hand of the LORD, as the rivers of water: he turneth it whithersoever he will. Every way of a man is right in his own eyes: but the LORD pondereth the hearts. To do justice and judgment is more acceptable to the LORD than sacrifice (Proverbs 21:1-3 KJV). Unto the upright there ariseth light in the darkness: he is gracious, and full of compassion, and righteous. A good man sheweth favour, and lendeth: he will guide his affairs with discretion. Surely he shall not be moved for ever: the righteous shall be in everlasting remembrance. He shall not be afraid of evil tidings: his heart is fixed, trusting in the LORD. His heart is established, he shall not be afraid, until he see his desire upon his enemies. He hath dispersed, he hath given to the poor; his righteousness endureth for ever; his horn shall be exalted with honour. The wicked shall see it, and be grieved; he shall gnash with his teeth, and melt away: the desire of the wicked shall perish (Psalm 112:4-10 KJV). The robbery of the wicked shall destroy them; because they refuse to do judgment (Proverbs 21:7 KJV).

Fruit of the Spirit: **Peace**

Luke 19:42 KJV

Saying, If thou hadst known, even thou, at least in this thy day, the things which belong unto thy peace! but now they are hid from thine eyes.

This is Madness

Opposing argument of reason almost took away my gladness.
I heard the "body" in dysfunction, which left me saying, "This is madness."

What is anger that's not righteous? Should I call it mad potential?
Eat the bread and drink the cup in a manner that's essential.

What kind of healing are they dodging when they won't accept the deep?
They get their rest with mindless chatter, but it's what's mindless that they reap.

They go on to speak of growth when it's their growth that has been stunted.
They go on with walking backwards while their blindness has been fronted.

They wouldn't recognize their faces if they were glancing in the mirror.
They boast of what they do while all the while they are a "hearer."

If double-talk was present, what was the knowledge that was missing?
What two words are represented as the two that's known for kissing?

Sometimes seeing has a way of producing what is sadness.
But when you look again, you will be overcome with gladness.

What's good about the light is that it shows what's called a badness.
Being mindful of His presence brings renewal from your madness.

This is Madness

Wherefore whosoever shall eat this bread, and drink this cup of the Lord, unworthily, shall be guilty of the body and blood of the Lord (1 Corinthians 11:27 KJV). An high look, and a proud heart, and the plowing of the wicked, is sin (Proverbs 21:4 KJV). The soul of the wicked desireth evil: his neighbour findeth no favour in his eyes (Proverbs 21:10 KJV). And the LORD said unto me, A conspiracy is found among the men of Judah, and among the inhabitants of Jerusalem. They are turned back to the iniquities of their forefathers, which refused to hear my words; and they went after other gods to serve them: the house of Israel and the house of Judah have broken my covenant which I made with their fathers. Therefore thus saith the LORD, Behold, I will bring evil upon them, which they shall not be able to escape; and though they shall cry unto me, I will not hearken unto them (Jeremiah 11:9-11 KJV).

In that day, saith the LORD, I will smite every horse with astonishment, and his rider with madness: and I will open mine eyes upon the house of Judah, and will smite every horse of the people with blindness. And the governors of Judah shall say in their heart, The inhabitants of Jerusalem shall be my strength in the LORD of hosts their God. In that day will I make the governors of Judah like an hearth of fire among the wood, and like a torch of fire in a sheaf; and they shall devour all the people round about, on the right hand and on the left: and Jerusalem shall be inhabited again in her own place, even in Jerusalem. The LORD also shall save the tents of Judah first, that the glory of the house of David and the glory of the inhabitants of Jerusalem do not magnify themselves against Judah. In that day shall the LORD defend the inhabitants of Jerusalem; and he that is feeble among them at that day shall be as David; and the house of David shall be as God, as the angel of the LORD before them. And it shall come to pass in that day, that I will seek to destroy all the nations that come against Jerusalem (Zechariah 12:4-9 KJV).

Unreal

They were titled pastor, but their shepherding unreal.
I was untitled for my boldness. What is the product of my zeal?

They were wounded by my words, and yet they claim to be the healers.
These hired men are thieves; they're also known as sheep stealers.

I couldn't believe they didn't get it! The deafness was unreal!
Their blindness on the matter mattered nothing to the deal.

Was my anger really pure, or was there sin within my heart?
Lord, let me run my business justly. From Your ways don't let me part.

They shake their heads at my decisions. My decisions' always yours.
They would see that they are holy and of You if one implores.

Perhaps they see it, and they know, but refuse to feel the shame.
The one's who served themselves were the ones who had first came.

They see a wolf when it is coming, but they cannot see their error.
Unreal judgments of a threat will surely make them run in terror.

With what degree did they act pious, hereby making faulty claims?
To what degree is my bow bent, in which my arrows are at aim?

Unreal

Verily, verily, I say unto you, He that entereth not by the door into the sheepfold, but climbeth up some other way, the same is a thief and a robber. But he that entereth in by the door is the shepherd of the sheep. To him the porter openeth; and the sheep hear his voice: and he calleth his own sheep by name, and leadeth them out. And when he putteth forth his own sheep, he goeth before them, and the sheep follow him: for they know his voice (John 10:1-4 KJV). I am the good shepherd: the good shepherd giveth his life for the sheep. But he that is an hireling, and not the shepherd, whose own the sheep are not, seeth the wolf coming, and leaveth the sheep, and fleeth: and the wolf catcheth them, and scattereth the sheep. The hireling fleeth, because he is an hireling, and careth not for the sheep (John 10:11-13 KJV). What hath my beloved to do in mine house, seeing she hath wrought lewdness with many, and the holy flesh is passed from thee? when thou doest evil, then thou rejoicest. The LORD called thy name, A green olive tree, fair, and of goodly fruit: with the noise of a great tumult he hath kindled fire upon it, and the branches of it are broken (Jeremiah 11:15-16 KJV).

For thus saith the LORD; We have heard a voice of trembling, of fear, and not of peace. Ask ye now, and see whether a man doth travail with child? wherefore do I see every man with his hands on his loins, as a woman in travail, and all faces are turned into paleness? Alas! for that day is great, so that none is like it: it is even the time of Jacob's trouble, but he shall be saved out of it. For it shall come to pass in that day, saith the LORD of hosts, that I will break his yoke from off thy neck, and will burst thy bonds, and strangers shall no more serve themselves of him: But they shall serve the LORD their God, and David their king, whom I will raise up unto them. Therefore fear thou not, O my servant Jacob, saith the LORD; neither be dismayed, O Israel: for, lo, I will save thee from afar, and thy seed from the land of their captivity; and Jacob shall return, and shall be in rest, and be quiet, and none shall make him afraid. For I am with thee, saith the LORD, to save thee: though I make a full end of all nations whither I have scattered thee, yet I will not make a full end of thee: but I will correct thee in measure, and will not leave thee altogether unpunished (Jeremiah 30:5-11 KJV).

Hear Me *Baa!*

I know that sheep are marked for slaughter.

They say stairs are for the wolves!

When have you ever heard of a sheep attacking wolves?

I also sat within the body, and I heard Him call some lions.

A den of thieves doesn't know this truth, because their truths don't come from Zion's.

He shut the lion's mouth; I mean, He shut the lion's trap!

Standing ovation for the humor! Yes, these hands are known to clap.

Their magic is to mischief as the "Ta" is to the "Da."

Those wolves didn't see this coming. He bent His bow, now hear me *baa!*

How does the sheepfold win in a race with deadly horses?

They conquer them with Jesus and with the heat of Life-ly forces.

Hear Me *Baa*!

They shall run like mighty men; they shall climb the wall like men of war; and they shall march every one on his ways, and they shall not break their ranks: Neither shall one thrust another; they shall walk every one in his path: and when they fall upon the sword, they shall not be wounded. They shall run to and fro in the city; they shall run upon the wall, they shall climb up upon the houses; they shall enter in at the windows like a thief. The earth shall quake before them; the heavens shall tremble: the sun and the moon shall be dark, and the stars shall withdraw their shining: And the LORD shall utter his voice before his army: for his camp is very great: for he is strong that executeth his word: for the day of the LORD is great and very terrible; and who can abide it (Joel 2:7-11 KJV)? Wherefore a lion out of the forest shall slay them, and a wolf of the evenings shall spoil them, a leopard shall watch over their cities: every one that goeth out thence shall be torn in pieces: because their transgressions are many, and their backslidings are increased (Jeremiah 5:6 KJV).

How shall I pardon thee for this? thy children have forsaken me, and sworn by them that are no gods: when I had fed them to the full, they then committed adultery, and assembled themselves by troops in the harlots' houses. They were as fed horses in the morning: every one neighed after his neighbour's wife. Shall I not visit for these things? saith the LORD: and shall not my soul be avenged on such a nation as this (Jeremiah 5:7-9 KJV)?" Oh that I had in the wilderness a lodging place of wayfaring men; that I might leave my people, and go from them! for they be all adulterers, an assembly of treacherous men. And they bend their tongues like their bow for lies: but they are not valiant for the truth upon the earth; for they proceed from evil to evil, and they know not me, saith the LORD (Jeremiah 9:2-3 KJV).

Serendipity

They are passing all these laws without knowing who they serve.
Yet there's nothing accidental in His plans to help you swerve.

How can they win a war, if they know not what they do?
Their will's not for perfection, but instead it's to pursue.

They're pursuing for a purpose that has been deemed to lose the fight.
They glory in a darkness that is known to pass for light.

Although they have great patience, it's not working with precise.
They answer to a "calling" without taking "good" advice.

Sons of lawlessness have an aim, but God's children are the arrows.
There's a shot at certain targets, and He's ~~with~~ width them, so He narrows.

How can they analyze a wind when I'm writing with an unction?
Who's acting on a whim that one would call executive function?

If they knew what they were doing, they wouldn't give themselves the credit.
They've booked that law to death, and who's to say they've ever read it?

What do they know about the Spirit and what It deems as authenticity?
They know nothing of its something, and I call it Serendipity.

Serendipity

I have done judgment and justice: leave me not to mine oppressors. Be surety for thy servant for good: let not the proud oppress me. Mine eyes fail for thy salvation, and for the word of thy righteousness. Deal with thy servant according unto thy mercy, and teach me thy statutes. I am thy servant; give me understanding, that I may know thy testimonies. It is time for thee, LORD, to work: for they have made void thy law. Therefore I love thy commandments above gold; yea, above fine gold. Therefore I esteem all thy precepts concerning all things to be right; and I hate every false way (Psalm 119:121-128 KJV). Princes have persecuted me without a cause: but my heart standeth in awe of thy word. I rejoice at thy word, as one that findeth great spoil. I hate and abhor lying: but thy law do I love (Psalm 119:161-163 KJV).

Great peace have they which love thy law: and nothing shall offend them. LORD, I have hoped for thy salvation, and done thy commandments. My soul hath kept thy testimonies; and I love them exceedingly. I have kept thy precepts and thy testimonies: for all my ways are before thee. Let my cry come near before thee, O LORD: give me understanding according to thy word. Let my supplication come before thee: deliver me according to thy word (Psalm 119:165-170 KJV). Keep not thou silence, O God: hold not thy peace, and be not still, O God. For, lo, thine enemies make a tumult: and they that hate thee have lifted up the head. They have taken crafty counsel against thy people, and consulted against thy hidden ones. They have said, Come, and let us cut them off from being a nation; that the name of Israel may be no more in remembrance. For they have consulted together with one consent: they are confederate against thee (Psalm 83:1-5 KJV).

Dust

My wording is a tongue! Eat your words or eat my dust!
I wouldn't offer my left hand, but my right hand says I must.

If my will has been exchanged, what is a will without the Hand?
It's a will that can't be tasted, which will's the produce of this land?

He remembers that we're dust, but He forgets the servants' sins.
To taste and see should be the focus. I left behind where stealth begins.

If sudden knowledge is destructive and denies your will to grow,
I 'll just leave your words alone and justly say that I don't know.

If a reader won't digest, how can she stomach being blind?
While my wisdom is distasteful, can't you still see I'm being kind?

Am I of the earth or has a certain kingdom come?
I do not know my debtors, and yes, now I'm playing dumb.

It's because I'm living Holy that I'm dusting off the fame.
You can't understand my judgment, because you do not know His name.

Dust

I am sought of them that asked not for me; I am found of them that sought me not: I said, Behold me, behold me, unto a nation that was not called by my name. I have spread out my hands all the day unto a rebellious people, which walketh in a way that was not good, after their own thoughts; A people that provoketh me to anger continually to my face; that sacrificeth in gardens, and burneth incense upon altars of brick (Isaiah 65:1-3 KJV). The tabernacles of robbers prosper, and they that provoke God are secure; into whose hand God bringeth abundantly. But ask now the beasts, and they shall teach thee; and the fowls of the air, and they shall tell thee: Or speak to the earth, and it shall teach thee: and the fishes of the sea shall declare unto thee. Who knoweth not in all these that the hand of the LORD hath wrought this (Job 12:6-9 KJV)?

In whose hand is the soul of every living thing, and the breath of all mankind. Doth not the ear try words? and the mouth taste his meat? With the ancient is wisdom; and in length of days understanding. With him is wisdom and strength, he hath counsel and understanding (Job 12:10-13 KJV). Behold, he withholdeth the waters, and they dry up: also he sendeth them out, and they overturn the earth. With him is strength and wisdom: the deceived and the deceiver are his (Job 12:15-16 KJV). He removeth away the speech of the trusty, and taketh away the understanding of the aged (Job 12:20 KJV). He increaseth the nations, and destroyeth them: he enlargeth the nations, and straiteneth them again (Job 12:23 KJV). The wolf and the lamb shall feed together, and the lion shall eat straw like the bullock: and dust shall be the serpent's meat. They shall not hurt nor destroy in all my holy mountain, saith the LORD (Isaiah 65:25 KJV)!"

Fringes

What if I told you that there was more than one kind of fringe?
There's one that leads to disaster, followed by a false holy trend.

They begin with a vision, and their garments end with tassels.
True holiness is mocked, because their hustle is of hassle.

They're handing out a heavy load, but they will not lift a finger.
Should royalties go to certain "kings" or the "writer" and the singer?

They think they have grown, all because they've grown in knowledge.
Yet, His wisdom teaches kingdom that you cannot get through college.

He's exalting His true servants. His true servants will be kings.
He's bringing low those once exalted, and it's with trembling He brings.

This classiness is daunting, and the statement's more than fact.
He's schooled the earthly wisdom with a perplexing class act.

Can you hear the kingdom speaking in the way that I'm denoting?
Can you see He offers freedom by the faith that He's promoting?

If you knew what you were doing, the truth would make you cringe.
His knowledge is worth seeking; in turn, you'll understand the fringe.

Fringes

Then spake Jesus to the multitude, and to his disciples, Saying The scribes and the Pharisees sit in Moses' seat: All therefore whatsoever they bid you observe, that observe and do; but do not ye after their works: for they say, and do not. For they bind heavy burdens and grievous to be borne, and lay them on men's shoulders; but they themselves will not move them with one of their fingers. But all their works they do for to be seen of men: they make broad their phylacteries, and enlarge the borders of their garments, And love the uppermost rooms at feasts, and the chief seats in the synagogues, And greetings in the markets, and to be called of men, Rabbi, Rabbi (Matthew 23:2-7 KJV).

And whosoever shall exalt himself shall be abased; and he that shall humble himself shall be exalted. But woe unto you, scribes and Pharisees, hypocrites! for ye shut up the kingdom of heaven against men: for ye neither go in yourselves, neither suffer ye them that are entering to go in. Woe unto you, scribes and Pharisees, hypocrites! for ye devour widows' houses, and for a pretence make long prayer: therefore ye shall receive the greater damnation. Woe unto you, scribes and Pharisees, hypocrites! for ye compass sea and land to make one proselyte, and when he is made, ye make him twofold more the child of hell than yourselves (Matthew 23:12-15 KJV)! The pillars of heaven tremble and are astonished at his reproof. He divideth the sea with his power, and by his understanding he smiteth through the proud. By his spirit he hath garnished the heavens; his hand hath formed the crooked serpent. Lo, these are parts of his ways: but how little a portion is heard of him? but the thunder of his power who can understand (Job 26:11-14 KJV)? For what is the hope of the hypocrite, though he hath gained, when God taketh away his soul? Will God hear his cry when trouble cometh upon him? Will he delight himself in the Almighty? will he always call upon God? I will teach you by the hand of God: that which is with the Almighty will I not conceal (Job 27:8-11 KJV).

Vengeful Acts

Rulers who knew the way, and new rulers who still don't.
I could say what's kind is vengeful, but subtle action says I won't

Sin will mock the sinner. Prophets analyze the acts.
They bite the hand that offers Bread and shake hands with life hacks.

This kind of thing, this kind of sting, will offer more than they can handle.
He turned the table; the tables turned. God has surely passed the mantle.

Who would think that a "blessing" could be a frightening vengeful act?
His love had always known just how the *body* would react.

If I could put it in a movie, I would call it *Sleeping Fallow.*
It would blind them with their truth, because their vision is that shallow.

They are known to leave a land in an uncultivated state.
They chastise an upright man, not to love him but to berate.

His true servants love to learn; they flourish in the courts of God.
The misruling of the wicked shall be met with an unsparing rod.

Vengeful Acts

Shall the throne of iniquity have fellowship with thee, which frameth mischief by a law? They gather themselves together against the soul of the righteous, and condemn the innocent blood. But the LORD is my defence; and my God is the rock of my refuge (Psalm 94:20-22 KJV). O Lord God, to whom vengeance belongeth; O God, to whom vengeance belongeth, shew thyself. Lift up thyself, thou judge of the earth: render a reward to the proud (Psalm 94:1-2 KJV). How long shall they utter and speak hard things? and all the workers of iniquity boast themselves? They break in pieces thy people, O LORD, and afflict thine heritage. They slay the widow and the stranger, and murder the fatherless. Yet they say, The LORD shall not see, neither shall the God of Jacob regard it (Psalm 94:4-7 KJV). He that chastiseth the heathen, shall not he correct? he that teacheth man knowledge, shall not he know? The LORD knoweth the thoughts of man, that they are vanity (Psalm 94:10-11 KJV).

How long, ye simple ones, will ye love simplicity? and the scorners delight in their scorning, and fools hate knowledge? Turn you at my reproof: behold, I will pour out my spirit unto you, I will make known my words unto you. Because I have called, and ye refused; I have stretched out my hand, and no man regarded; But ye have set at nought all my counsel, and would none of my reproof: I also will laugh at your calamity; I will mock when your fear cometh; When your fear cometh as desolation, and your destruction cometh as a whirlwind; when distress and anguish cometh upon you (Proverbs 1:22-27 KJV)? For that they hated knowledge, and did not choose the fear of the LORD: They would none of my counsel: they despised all my reproof. Therefore shall they eat of the fruit of their own way, and be filled with their own devices. For the turning away of the simple shall slay them, and the prosperity of fools shall destroy them (Proverbs 1:29-32 KJV)."

Fresh Wickedness

New Foolishness is funny. The joke's always on you.
Fresh wickedness is rampant. Unfair gain denies the few.

The few who truly followed were the servants that they had mocked.
Their hollowness was branded by the substance that had docked.

They were vengeful in their acts. They tried to make the kingdom theirs.
They didn't know that what they planted was always representing tares.

Look how sin has mocked the sinner. The mocking can be seen.
Yet they're blinded by what mocks them, and their actions weren't too keen.

Who's keen on getting wisdom? Who's keen on understanding law?
Vague demands are what you get as nations' wounds are showing raw.

Insight: Isaiah 1:6

What are servants without process or without a healing oil?
I've seen a wicked man with power flourish in his native soil.

Psalm 37:35 AMP

Psalm 29:8 AMP

The LORD is shaking the wilderness; the wilderness of Kadesh.
This is a teaching rain; its stormy coming will refresh.

Deuteronomy 32:2 AMP

Fresh Wickedness

Thou makest us a reproach to our neighbours, a scorn and a derision to them that are round about us. Thou makest us a byword among the heathen, a shaking of the head among the people. My confusion is continually before me, and the shame of my face hath covered me, For the voice of him that reproacheth and blasphemeth; by reason of the enemy and avenger (Psalm 44:13-16 KJV). Wherefore hear the word of the LORD, ye scornful men, that rule this people which is in Jerusalem. Because ye have said, We have made a covenant with death, and with hell are we at agreement; when the overflowing scourge shall pass through, it shall not come unto us: for we have made lies our refuge, and under falsehood have we hid ourselves: Therefore thus saith the Lord GOD, Behold, I lay in Zion for a foundation a stone, a tried stone, a precious corner stone, a sure foundation: he that believeth shall not make haste (Isaiah 28:14-16 KJV).

For the LORD shall rise up as in mount Perazim, he shall be wroth as in the valley of Gibeon, that he may do his work, his strange work; and bring to pass his act, his strange act. Now therefore be ye not mockers, lest your bands be made strong: for I have heard from the Lord GOD of hosts a consumption, even determined upon the whole earth (Isaiah 28:21-22 KJV). Give ye ear, and hear my voice; hearken, and hear my speech. When he hath made plain the face thereof, doth he not cast abroad the fitches, and scatter the cummin, and cast in the principal wheat and the appointed barley and the rie in their place? For the fitches are not threshed with a threshing instrument, neither is a cart wheel turned about upon the cummin; but the fitches are beaten out with a staff, and the cummin with a rod. This also cometh forth from the LORD of hosts, which is wonderful in counsel, and excellent in working (Isaiah 28:23, 25, 27, 29 KJV).

Disdainful Glances

I sometimes listened before knowing the place of where that someone stands.
I received His revelation within the darkness of His plans.

I didn't have exacting knowledge; therefore, my wisdom was enhanced.
I saw the truth of what He knew, in which I never would have glanced.

Life was hanging in the balance, but without a second chance.
Although a life was present, what's holy didn't take its stance.

Timing was a factor. Wholeness had to be restored.
I was killed by what I saw within that life that was adored.

I posted based on image, not for political astuteness.
Comments weren't without disdain; their glances came without acuteness.

Some will look at truth disgusted. Some fail to eat His humble pie.
They have failed to taste and see, and so they cannot shake the lie.

Who's more defensive than discerning? Perhaps they're called the shepherds.
They can't distinguish between the lion, nor the grizzly, or the leopard.

What kind of worship blinds the eyes and then claims to get a glance?
Worship without the Son keeps them in a corporate trance.

Disdainful Glances

The young lions do lack, and suffer hunger: but they that seek the LORD shall not want any good thing. Come, ye children, hearken unto me: I will teach you the fear of the LORD (Psalm 34:10-11 KJV). Man that is in honour, and understandeth not, is like the beasts that perish (Psalm 49:20 KJV). And the beast which I saw was like unto a leopard, and his feet were as the feet of a bear, and his mouth as the mouth of a lion: and the dragon gave him his power, and his seat, and great authority. And I saw one of his heads as it were wounded to death; and his deadly wound was healed: and all the world wondered after the beast. And they worshipped the dragon which gave power unto the beast: and they worshipped the beast, saying, Who is like unto the beast? who is able to make war with him (Revelation 13:2-4 KJV)? The LORD shall make the rain of thy land powder and dust: from heaven shall it come down upon thee, until thou be destroyed (Deuteronomy 28:24 KJV). And thy heaven that is over thy head shall be brass, and the earth that is under thee shall be iron (Deuteronomy 28:23 KJV).

And there was given unto him a mouth speaking great things and blasphemies; and power was given unto him to continue forty and two months. And he opened his mouth in blasphemy against God, to blaspheme his name, and his tabernacle, and them that dwell in heaven. And it was given unto him to make war with the saints, and to overcome them: and power was given him over all kindreds, and tongues, and nations. And all that dwell upon the earth shall worship him, whose names are not written in the book of life of the Lamb slain from the foundation of the world. If any man have an ear, let him hear. He that leadeth into captivity shall go into captivity: he that killeth with the sword must be killed with the sword. Here is the patience and the faith of the saints (Revelation 13:5-10 KJV). The LORD shall open unto thee his good treasure, the heaven to give the rain unto thy land in his season, and to bless all the work of thine hand: and thou shalt lend unto many nations, and thou shalt not borrow (Deuteronomy 28:12 KJV).

Fruit of the Spirit: **Temperance**

He that hath no rule over his own spirit is like a city that is broken down, and without walls (Proverbs 25:28 KJV).

Learn the Stroke

What is this that I'm seeing? Have I done all of this for nothing?
He crowned me with His wealth, and it appeared to add to nothing.

I remained within His will, yet certain riches said I won't.
Simple ways make other offers; they claim to serve Him, but they don't.

This stroke is known as painful and can make you feel confused.
It's known to pen you in as if the pen is being misused.

Ignorance and confusion, could you stand to learn the difference?
I was sitting at His feet, and I learned the truth by Inference.

Like a pen that's out of ink, I was feeling drained and useless.
The process was perplexing, and it seemed to be so ruthless.

What is a ruthless expedition under caring hands that guide?
My pen has learned the stroke, and it marks the course in stride.

Learn the Stroke

That I may perform the oath which I have sworn unto your fathers, to give them a land flowing with milk and honey, as it is this day. Then answered I, and said, So be it, O LORD. Then the LORD said unto me, Proclaim all these words in the cities of Judah, and in the streets of Jerusalem, saying, Hear ye the words of this covenant, and do them. For I earnestly protested unto your fathers in the day that I brought them up out of the land of Egypt, even unto this day, rising early and protesting, saying, Obey my voice. Yet they obeyed not, nor inclined their ear, but walked every one in the imagination of their evil heart: therefore I will bring upon them all the words of this covenant, which I commanded them to do: but they did them not. And the LORD said unto me, A conspiracy is found among the men of Judah, and among the inhabitants of Jerusalem. They are turned back to the iniquities of their forefathers, which refused to hear my words; and they went after other gods to serve them: the house of Israel and the house of Judah have broken my covenant which I made with their fathers (Jeremiah 11:5-10 KJV)?

The LORD called thy name, A green olive tree, fair, and of goodly fruit: with the noise of a great tumult he hath kindled fire upon it, and the branches of it are broken (Jeremiah 11:16 KJV). Open thy doors, O Lebanon, that the fire may devour thy cedars. Howl, fir tree; for the cedar is fallen; because the mighty are spoiled: howl, O ye oaks of Bashan; for the forest of the vintage is come down (Zechariah 11:1-2 KJV)! Thus speaketh the LORD of hosts, saying, Execute true judgment, and shew mercy and compassions every man to his brother: And oppress not the widow, nor the fatherless, the stranger, nor the poor; and let none of you imagine evil against his brother in your heart. But they refused to hearken, and pulled away the shoulder, and stopped their ears, that they should not hear. Yea, they made their hearts as an adamant stone, lest they should hear the law, and the words which the LORD of hosts hath sent in his spirit by the former prophets: therefore came a great wrath from the LORD of hosts (Zechariah 7:9-12 KJV).

Self-Control

I was feeling like a sinking ship, but the Lord, He spoke His peace.
He said, "I put you in this storm." I'll say His comfort never ceased.

I was feeling weak and wicked. My emotions were unstable.
I cried out about my thoughts; He kept whispering that I am able.

I felt like I was doomed, like I was failing under pressure.
He elevated what was sound, but I didn't know the stressors.

Do I love, or do I lust? Lord, these feelings are conflicting.
I'd love to have my cravings, but my lust is so restricting.

I was getting on my nerves, because I didn't know my secret.
I would win the war for love if my failures were to leak it.

I had to mortify my members making dew from what was dry.
I flirted with disaster while being the apple of His eye.

What kind of tree is of this fruit? Some say an apple, but it is not.
I'm a blemish on your ways if you can understand my spot.

Self-Control

Purge me with hyssop, and I shall be clean: wash me, and I shall be whiter than snow. Make me to hear joy and gladness; that the bones which thou hast broken may rejoice. Hide thy face from my sins, and blot out all mine iniquities. Create in me a clean heart, O God; and renew a right spirit within me. Cast me not away from thy presence; and take not thy holy spirit from me. Restore unto me the joy of thy salvation; and uphold me with thy free spirit. Then will I teach transgressors thy ways; and sinners shall be converted unto thee. Deliver me from bloodguiltiness, O God, thou God of my salvation: and my tongue shall sing aloud of thy righteousness. O LORD, open thou my lips; and my mouth shall shew forth thy praise. For thou desirest not sacrifice; else would I give it: thou delightest not in burnt offering. The sacrifices of God are a broken spirit: a broken and a contrite heart, O God, thou wilt not despise (Psalms 51:7-17 KJV).

Do good in thy good pleasure unto Zion: build thou the walls of Jerusalem (Psalm 51:18 KJV). Have mercy upon me, O God, according to thy lovingkindness: according unto the multitude of thy tender mercies blot out my transgressions. Wash me throughly from mine iniquity, and cleanse me from my sin. For I acknowledge my transgressions: and my sin is ever before me. Against thee, thee only, have I sinned, and done this evil in thy sight: that thou mightest be justified when thou speakest, and be clear when thou judgest. Behold, I was shapen in iniquity; and in sin did my mother conceive me. Behold, thou desirest truth in the inward parts: and in the hidden part thou shalt make me to know wisdom (Psalm 51:1-6 KJV). As the apple tree among the trees of the wood, so is my beloved among the sons. I sat down under his shadow with great delight, and his fruit was sweet to my taste. He brought me to the banqueting house, and his banner over me was love. Stay me with flagons, comfort me with apples: for I am sick of love. His left hand is under my head, and his right hand doth embrace me (Song of Solomon 2:3-6 KJV).

Pitfalls of Obedience

I ran into a pitfall after running a command.
What I thought would be exciting didn't match the better plan.

I was confounded at the outcome; my time was spent to say the least.
I was not happy with the Lord. Life didn't seem a continual feast.

What is promoting with demotion, but restoration of one's youth.
"Good things" can be more troubling, if you want to know the truth.

What is satisfaction if it doesn't please my soul?
It never passes up an age, but always times another goal.

I couldn't see the point. I couldn't hear Him past my screams.
Righteous indignation isn't always what it seems.

My heart was overwhelmed. I held back my eyes from tears.
I was alarmed at how the process had revealed my anxious fears.

While being absentminded, He made me mindful of His presence.
When I shared my anxious thoughts, He deemed it amity in its essence.

Pitfalls of Obedience

He raiseth up the poor out of the dust, and lifteth the needy out of the dunghill (Psalm 113:7 KJV). Thou knowest that I am not wicked; and there is none that can deliver out of thine hand. Thine hands have made me and fashioned me together round about; yet thou dost destroy me (Job 10:7-8 KJV). Have mercy upon me, O God, according to thy lovingkindness: according unto the multitude of thy tender mercies blot out my transgressions. Wash me throughly from mine iniquity, and cleanse me from my sin. For I acknowledge my transgressions: and my sin is ever before me. Against thee, thee only, have I sinned, and done this evil in thy sight: that thou mightest be justified when thou speakest, and be clear when thou judgest. Behold, I was shapen in iniquity; and in sin did my mother conceive me. Behold, thou desirest truth in the inward parts: and in the hidden part thou shalt make me to know wisdom. Purge me with hyssop, and I shall be clean: wash me, and I shall be whiter than snow (Psalm 51:1-7 KJV).

Make me to hear joy and gladness; that the bones which thou hast broken may rejoice. Hide thy face from my sins, and blot out all mine iniquities. Create in me a clean heart, O God; and renew a right spirit within me. Cast me not away from thy presence; and take not thy holy spirit from me. Restore unto me the joy of thy salvation; and uphold me with thy free spirit. Then will I teach transgressors thy ways; and sinners shall be converted unto thee. Deliver me from bloodguiltiness, O God, thou God of my salvation: and my tongue shall sing aloud of thy righteousness. O LORD, open thou my lips; and my mouth shall shew forth thy praise. For thou desirest not sacrifice; else would I give it: thou delightest not in burnt offering (Psalm 51:8-16 KJV). …where I heard a language that I understood not. I removed his shoulder from the burden: his hands were delivered from the pots (Psalm 81:5-6 KJV).

No Hands!

He led me not into temptation but delivered me from evil.
I obeyed a rare command, and it caused a great upheaval.

Some would say that I rebelled. Some would have called it of the devil!
They may have seen it as a sin, because they haven't reached this level.

He knew that I'd be tempted and that my mind would get confused.
The opposite sex became my friend; it was the friendship that was used.

It was used to help shine light and to demonstrate the truth.
Yet they would rather dwell in darkness if it meant that there's no proof.

My wilderness was invented by the mighty hand of God.
He humbled my hands at work and now I will lead them with a rod.

I was quickened by His wisdom and by sudden reprimands.
I was delivered from types of evil with no laying on of hands.

No Hands

Who shall ascend into the hill of the LORD? or who shall stand in his holy place? He that hath clean hands, and a pure heart; who hath not lifted up his soul unto vanity, nor sworn deceitfully (Psalm 24:3-4 KJV). Sing aloud unto God our strength: make a joyful noise unto the God of Jacob. Take a psalm, and bring hither the timbrel, the pleasant harp with the psaltery. Blow up the trumpet in the new moon, in the time appointed, on our solemn feast day. For this was a statute for Israel, and a law of the God of Jacob. This he ordained in Joseph for a testimony, when he went out through the land of Egypt: where I heard a language that I understood not (Psalm 81:1-5 KJV).

Thou calledst in trouble, and I delivered thee; I answered thee in the secret place of thunder: I proved thee at the waters of Meribah. Selah. Hear, O my people, and I will testify unto thee: O Israel, if thou wilt hearken unto me; There shall no strange god be in thee; neither shalt thou worship any strange god. I am the LORD thy God, which brought thee out of the land of Egypt: open thy mouth wide, and I will fill it. But my people would not hearken to my voice; and Israel would none of me. So I gave them up unto their own hearts' lust: and they walked in their own counsels. Oh that my people had hearkened unto me, and Israel had walked in my ways! I should soon have subdued their enemies, and turned my hand against their adversaries. The haters of the LORD should have submitted themselves unto him: but their time should have endured for ever. He should have fed them also with the finest of the wheat: and with honey out of the rock should I have satisfied thee (Psalm 81:7-16 KJV)! Blessed be the LORD my strength which teacheth my hands to war, and my fingers to fight: My goodness, and my fortress; my high tower, and my deliverer; my shield, and he in whom I trust; who subdueth my people under me (Psalm 144:1-2 KJV).

Patience with Riddles

Be careful of My timing; my thumbs are known to twiddle.
A quick reference to an answer leaves me questioning the riddle.

Which truths are sounding like a question? Should I be perfect and entire?
The choice is up to you, which draws the consequences nigher.

What were my temptations that I should count it all a joy?
Perhaps I'm counting my degree, now you can say I'm being coy.

Was this concupiscence of Satan, or was it born of my own lust?
If two can play this game, well, then which loss should be the must?

He exposed me to my lust; my temptations were enduring.
The richness of what flattered made the offers more alluring.

If wisdom should expose you, well, then blessed is the man.
He led me "foolishly" to death, and I say blessed is the plan.

This conundrum left me feeling like anything but glorifying,
A main "member" to a standard without my members mortifying.

Patience with Riddles

For as I passed by, and beheld your devotions, I found an altar with this inscription, To The Unknown God. Whom therefore ye ignorantly worship, him declare I unto you. God that made the world and all things therein, seeing that he is Lord of heaven and earth, dwelleth not in temples made with hands; Neither is worshipped with men's hands, as though he needed any thing, seeing he giveth to all life, and breath, and all things; And hath made of one blood all nations of men for to dwell on all the face of the earth, and hath determined the times before appointed, and the bounds of their habitation (Acts 17:23-26 KJV). Therefore judge nothing before the time, until the Lord come, who both will bring to light the hidden things of darkness, and will make manifest the counsels of the hearts: and then shall every man have praise of God (1 Corinthians 4:5 KJV).

Let a man so account of us, as of the ministers of Christ, and stewards of the mysteries of God. Moreover it is required in stewards, that a man be found faithful. But with me it is a very small thing that I should be judged of you, or of man's judgment: yea, I judge not mine own self. For I know nothing by myself; yet am I not hereby justified: but he that judgeth me is the Lord (1 Corinthians 4:1-4 KJV). For this cause have I sent unto you Timotheus, who is my beloved son, and faithful in the Lord, who shall bring you into remembrance of my ways which be in Christ, as I teach every where in every church (1 Corinthians 4:17 KJV). Then shalt thou understand righteousness, and judgment, and equity; yea, every good path (Proverbs 2:9 KJV).

Cherry-Pickers

They need me and my ways, but they want me in another.
I know they want to "pop my cherry," my legs one over the other.

Insight: Proverbs 26:7 ASV

They seek and hope I do, to do what I have never done.
It started with a struggle; now my new way has just begun.

I'm showing you my path; therefore, I'm speaking what I've walked.
I've picked the purest language; now I'm writing what we've talked.

What about this speech would make a servant mortified?
I'm walking out the Word. My steps are more than fortified.

Wickedness is what it is, and there's no way around it.
Wisdom is what it's not, and it's got you surrounded.

Their ears have tried my words, but they couldn't read my lips.
The synagogues of Satan have been known to flog with whips.

What is a twisted tongue but a fence that will not mend?
It is a tongue that picks itself. It picks itself to its own end.

Cherry-Pickers

Wherefore lay apart all filthiness and superfluity of naughtiness, and receive with meekness the engrafted word, which is able to save your souls. But be ye doers of the word, and not hearers only, deceiving your own selves.For if any be a hearer of the word, and not a doer, he is like unto a man beholding his natural face in a glass: For he beholdeth himself, and goeth his way, and straightway forgetteth what manner of man he was. But whoso looketh into the perfect law of liberty, and continueth therein, he being not a forgetful hearer, but a doer of the work, this man shall be blessed in his deed. If any man among you seem to be religious, and bridleth not his tongue, but deceiveth his own heart, this man's religion is vain. Pure religion and undefiled before God and the Father is this, To visit the fatherless and widows in their affliction, and to keep himself unspotted from the world (James 1:21-27 KJV).

The meek will he guide in judgment: and the meek will he teach his way. All the paths of the LORD are mercy and truth unto such as keep his covenant and his testimonies. For thy name's sake, O LORD, pardon mine iniquity; for it is great. What man is he that feareth the LORD? him shall he teach in the way that he shall choose. The secret of the LORD is with them that fear him; and he will shew them his covenant (Psalm 25:9-10, 12, 14 KJV). Before destruction the heart of man is haughty, and before honour is humility. He that answereth a matter before he heareth it, it is folly and shame unto him (Proverbs 18:12-13 KJV). Should a wise man utter vain knowledge, and fill his belly with the east wind? Should he reason with unprofitable talk? or with speeches wherewith he can do no good? Yea, thou castest off fear, and restrainest prayer before God. For thy mouth uttereth thine iniquity, and thou choosest the tongue of the crafty. Thine own mouth condemneth thee, and not I: yea, thine own lips testify against thee (Job 15:2-6 KJV). The righteous eateth to the satisfying of his soul: but the belly of the wicked shall want (Proverbs 13:25 KJV).

Beast-Like Belly

His glory met my weakness; My thoughts are less than wordy.
I write of mockery in riddles. Should they blame it on the birdie?

You reap what you sow. What goes around comes around.
Karma cannot handle seeing, so what hits one turns back around.

Homographic explanations are the waters of a sameness.
Which river offers deadly water yet flows with character that's shameless?

Proverbs 24:17 AMP
Certain sowing looks for justice; Karma looks to laugh.
He stuck it to me "good," and now I'm leading with a staff.

My tongue was set on fire, and they tried to extinguish.
If my tongue is of His water, certain fire will distinguish.

The light can be a burden. The yoke reveals a hardness.
What is hidden about my troubles that is likened to a harness?

If I'm not a senseless horse, what am I, to say the least?
I'm a calculated risk that solves the meaning of the beast.

Real truth is not for "death," so death puts it up for auction.
I've purchased what is rare, and therefore, failure's not an option.

Beast-Like Belly

Bread of deceit is sweet to a man; but afterwards his mouth shall be filled with gravel (Proverbs 20:17 KJV). A man's belly shall be satisfied with the fruit of his mouth; and with the increase of his lips shall he be filled (Proverbs 18:20 KJV). Praise ye the LORD. Praise, O ye servants of the LORD, praise the name of the LORD. Blessed be the name of the LORD from this time forth and for evermore. From the rising of the sun unto the going down of the same the LORD's name is to be praised. The LORD is high above all nations, and his glory above the heavens. Who is like unto the LORD our God, who dwelleth on high, Who humbleth himself to behold the things that are in heaven, and in the earth (Psalm 113:1-6 KJV). Do ye indeed speak righteousness, O congregation? do ye judge uprightly, O ye sons of men? Yea, in heart ye work wickedness; ye weigh the violence of your hands in the earth. The wicked are estranged from the womb: they go astray as soon as they be born, speaking lies (Psalm 58:1-3 KJV).

Fools make a mock at sin: but among the righteous there is favour (Proverbs 14:9 KJV). And they will deceive every one his neighbour, and will not speak the truth: they have taught their tongue to speak lies, and weary themselves to commit iniquity. And they bend their tongues like their bow for lies: but they are not valiant for the truth upon the earth; for they proceed from evil to evil, and they know not me, saith the LORD (Jeremiah 9:5, 3 KJV). The righteous shall rejoice when he seeth the vengeance: he shall wash his feet in the blood of the wicked. So that a man shall say, Verily there is a reward for the righteous: verily he is a God that judgeth in the earth (Psalm 58:10-11 KJV)." That he may set him with princes, even with the princes of his people. He maketh the barren woman to keep house, and to be a joyful mother of children. Praise ye the LORD (Psalm 113:8-9 KJV)!

Rime Rhymes

Whoever thought that ice could flow like a river?
The river is so cold that it will make you quiver.

Quiver with fear when you hear,
What the rhyme is saying.
It's steadily focused, readily praying,
For the righteous to flow correctly.
They help the lost become erectly,
Positioned to become more than they ever dreamed,
They'll find out that an abundant life is what He deemed
for those who love Him,
And for those who show them,
How His rhymes can turn rime into anything.

Rime Rhymes

Therefore will not we fear, though the earth be removed, and though the mountains be carried into the midst of the sea; Though the waters thereof roar and be troubled, though the mountains shake with the swelling thereof. Selah. There is a river, the streams whereof shall make glad the city of God, the holy place of the tabernacles of the most High. God is in the midst of her; she shall not be moved: God shall help her, and that right early. The heathen raged, the kingdoms were moved: he uttered his voice, the earth melted. The LORD of hosts is with us; the God of Jacob is our refuge. Selah. Come, behold the works of the LORD, what desolations he hath made in the earth. He maketh wars to cease unto the end of the earth; he breaketh the bow, and cutteth the spear in sunder; he burneth the chariot in the fire. Be still, and know that I am God: I will be exalted among the heathen, I will be exalted in the earth. The LORD of hosts is with us; the God of Jacob is our refuge. Selah (Psalm 46:1-11 KJV).

The LORD lifteth up the meek: he casteth the wicked down to the ground. Sing unto the LORD with thanksgiving; sing praise upon the harp unto our God: Who covereth the heaven with clouds, who prepareth rain for the earth, who maketh grass to grow upon the mountains (Psalm 147:6-8 KJV). By the breath of God frost is given: and the breadth of the waters is straitened (Job 37:10 KJV). Out of whose womb came the ice? and the hoary frost of heaven, who hath gendered it (Job 38:29 KJV)? He sendeth forth his commandment upon earth: his word runneth very swiftly. He giveth snow like wool: he scattereth the hoarfrost like ashes. He casteth forth his ice like morsels: who can stand before his cold? He sendeth out his word, and melteth them: he causeth his wind to blow, and the waters flow. He sheweth his word unto Jacob, his statutes and his judgments unto Israel. He hath not dealt so with any nation: and as for his judgments, they have not known them. Praise ye the LORD (Psalm 147:15-20 KJV).

One Sip

Why would Jesus fill your cup and then command to take one sip?
Would you lose your footing if I let the answer slip?

I understood why they got drunk. I sipped with a loosened grip.
I pieced together what they wouldn't. What is a side without a flip?

Is He an "Indian giver," taking advantage of certain settlers?
He settled the matter with His authority, and He gave it to the mettlers.

Are you about your Father's business, or in the business on your own?
My "tree" has been deemed good, and so the light has just been shown.

My works have been established; they're tested by the Holy Spirit.
The drunken fear my skill. Accusers claim they're testing spirits.

Lord, I don't want to be a robber. Teach me how to be a teller.
You've taught me when to act on faith, and my performance will be stellar.

Their ideas of the matter have been revealed and pass for sentries.
Their methods have been known to kill and steal for more than centuries.

One Sip

Mine heart within me is broken because of the prophets; all my bones shake; I am like a drunken man, and like a man whom wine hath overcome, because of the LORD, and because of the words of his holiness. For the land is full of adulterers; for because of swearing the land mourneth; the pleasant places of the wilderness are dried up, and their course is evil, and their force is not right (Jeremiah 23:9-10 KJV). In the same day also will I punish all those that leap on the threshold, which fill their masters' houses with violence and deceit. Howl, ye inhabitants of Maktesh, for all the merchant people are cut down; all they that bear silver are cut off. And it shall come to pass at that time, that I will search Jerusalem with candles, and punish the men that are settled on their lees: that say in their heart, The LORD will not do good, neither will he do evil (Zephaniah 1:9, 11-12 KJV).

Therefore their goods shall become a booty, and their houses a desolation: they shall also build houses, but not inhabit them; and they shall plant vineyards, but not drink the wine thereof. The great day of the LORD is near, it is near, and hasteth greatly, even the voice of the day of the LORD: the mighty man shall cry there bitterly (Zephaniah 1:13-14 KJV). Woe unto him that giveth his neighbour drink, that puttest thy bottle to him, and makest him drunken also, that thou mayest look on their nakedness! Thou art filled with shame for glory: drink thou also, and let thy foreskin be uncovered: the cup of the LORD's right hand shall be turned unto thee, and shameful spewing shall be on thy glory (Habakkuk 2:15-16 KJV).

Harm

What is this thing called harm that the Saints were meant to slay?
There is a path that seems right, but He calls it harm's way.

Faithful witnesses are rare; who'll use the word as an accuser?
When ignorance plays a role, it uses truth as an abuser.

Humiliation will find His enemies; their shame will cover like a cloak.
While I was serving in the temple, I became the inside/outside joke.

The wolves are crying out. The wolves are filled with terror.
There are miscarriages of justice through a type-two error.

His understanding of the matter is called a choice pearl.
Protectionism passes by with what intent but to imperil?

Whoever tries to save will lose; those who lose shall surely save.
Those who misapply His truths shall be known to rant and rave.

Who are our neighbors? Are they close by? Are they of other nations?
How can I relay a truth relating separatisms vast relations?

Harm

He that is unjust, let him be unjust still: and he which is filthy, let him be filthy still: and he that is righteous, let him be righteous still: and he that is holy, let him be holy still (Revelation 22:11 KJV)." Behold, I send you forth as sheep in the midst of wolves: be ye therefore wise as serpents, and harmless as doves. But beware of men: for they will deliver you up to the councils, and they will scourge you in their synagogues; And ye shall be brought before governors and kings for my sake, for a testimony against them and the Gentiles. But when they deliver you up, take no thought how or what ye shall speak: for it shall be given you in that same hour what ye shall speak. For it is not ye that speak, but the Spirit of your Father which speaketh in you (Matthew 10:16-20 KJV).

And the brother shall deliver up the brother to death, and the father the child: and the children shall rise up against their parents, and cause them to be put to death. And ye shall be hated of all men for my name's sake: but he that endureth to the end shall be saved (Matthew 10:21-22 KJV). And into whatsoever city or town ye shall enter, enquire who in it is worthy; and there abide till ye go thence. And when ye come into an house, salute it. And if the house be worthy, let your peace come upon it: but if it be not worthy, let your peace return to you. And whosoever shall not receive you, nor hear your words, when ye depart out of that house or city, shake off the dust of your feet. Verily I say unto you, It shall be more tolerable for the land of Sodom and Gomorrha in the day of judgment, than for that city (Matthew 10:11-15 KJV).

The Last ~~Ditch~~ Stitch

Insight: Zechariah 5:6-8 TLB

The foolish servants put all their eggs in one basket.

They traded life for death, and it led them to their casket.

What's the opposite of wisdom? I thought it was the fool.

Time and again He measured; He knew when wickedness would rule.

They are known to offer bribes to whoever falsely swears.

This is a last stitch effort, and it's showing that He cares.

There is justice underway. Is this a war of words?

Corrupt decisions from the godly not looking well unto thy herds.

Proverbs 27:23 KJV

The wolves rejected peace; I saw the war within their hearts.

They work to hide their ambush, and He knows it, so He parts.

Proverbs 31:19 NLT

My hands were busy spinning thread; my fingers twisting fiber.

I used the threading for His purpose; now the foes(s) a toothless tiger.

Matthew 10:16 AMP

I was as wise as a serpent; I was as innocent as a dove.

What looked like harm approaching was a war brought forth from love.

That Last ~~Ditch~~ Stitch

Be thou diligent to know the state of thy flocks, and look well to thy herds (Proverbs 27:23 KJV). Thou shalt not wrest judgment; thou shalt not respect persons, neither take a gift: for a gift doth blind the eyes of the wise, and pervert the words of the righteous (Deuteronomy 16:19 KJV). Hear the right, O LORD, attend unto my cry, give ear unto my prayer, that goeth not out of feigned lips (Psalm 17:1 KJV). Keep me as the apple of the eye, hide me under the shadow of thy wings, From the wicked that oppress me, from my deadly enemies, who compass me about. They are inclosed in their own fat: with their mouth they speak proudly (Psalm 17:8-10 KJV). They have now compassed us in our steps: they have set their eyes bowing down to the earth; Like as a lion that is greedy of his prey, and as it were a young lion lurking in secret places. Arise, O LORD, disappoint him, cast him down: deliver my soul from the wicked, which is thy sword (Psalm 17:13 KJV).

If thou seest the oppression of the poor, and violent perverting of judgment and justice in a province, marvel not at the matter: for he that is higher than the highest regardeth; and there be higher than they (Ecclesiastes 5:8 KJV). Break their teeth, O God, in their mouth: break out the great teeth of the young lions, O LORD. Let them melt away as waters which run continually: when he bendeth his bow to shoot his arrows, let them be as cut in pieces. As a snail which melteth, let every one of them pass away: like the untimely birth of a woman, that they may not see the sun. Before your pots can feel the thorns, he shall take them away as with a whirlwind, both living, and in his wrath (Psalm 58:6-9 KJV)! I will bring it forth, saith the LORD of hosts, and it shall enter into the house of the thief, and into the house of him that sweareth falsely by my name: and it shall remain in the midst of his house, and shall consume it with the timber thereof and the stones thereof (Zechariah 5:4 KJV)."

To Contact the Author,

Please Write:

P.O. Box 58760

Louisville KY. 40268

www.ingramcontent.com/pod-product-compliance
Lightning Source LLC
LaVergne TN
LVHW061223060426
835509LV00012B/1395